BIBLE KEY WORDS

IV. RIGHTEOUSNESS

MANUALS FROM KITTEL

Translated and edited by

J. R. COATES

BIBLE KEY WORDS
FROM GERHARD KITTEL'S
*THEOLOGISCHES WÖRTERBUCH
ZUM NEUEN TESTAMENT*

RIGHTEOUSNESS

BY

GOTTFRIED QUELL &
GOTTLOB SCHRENK

LONDON
ADAM AND CHARLES BLACK
SOHO SQUARE

THIS EDITION FIRST PUBLISHED 1951
BY A. AND C. BLACK LIMITED
4, 5 AND 6 SOHO SQUARE LONDON W.1

Translated from the German
first edition, Stuttgart, 1935
and with additional notes
by J. R. Coates

MADE IN GREAT BRITAIN
PRINTED AT THE UNIVERSITY PRESS
ABERDEEN

PREFACE

THE quarrel of the world to-day is not so much between right and wrong as between rival ways of defining and doing right, and this points to the underlying unity of mankind. The concept of righteousness is a vital part of the ultimate mystery of man as a social and individual being, and also a clear mark of his capacity for pure worship. But every man experiences frustration and failure, a sense, however faint and fitful, of fundamental guilt and unrighteousness.

That is why the Bible is our Gospel. Matthew Arnold wrote truly in the preface to a cheaper edition of *Literature and Dogma* : " The subject of the Old Testament, Salvation by righteousness, the subject of the New, Righteousness by Jesus Christ, are, in positive strict truth, man's most momentous matters of concern ". But he failed to appreciate the root of the matter, as understood by Paul. This was stated with much warmth and simplicity by an unknown apologist of the second century : " When our iniquity had been fully accomplished, and it had been made perfectly manifest that punishment and death were expected as its recompense, and the season came which God had ordained, when henceforth he should manifest his goodness and power (O the exceeding great kindness and love of God), he hated us not, neither rejected us, nor bore us malice, but was longsuffering and patient, and in pity for us took upon himself our sins, and himself parted with his own son as a ransom for us, the holy for the lawless, the guileless for the evil, the just for the unjust, the incorruptible for the corruptible,

v

the immortal for the mortal. For what else but his righteousness would have covered our sins ? In whom was it possible for us lawless and ungodly men to have been justified, save only in the son of God ? O the sweet exchange, O the inscrutable creation, O the unexpected benefits ; that the iniquity of many should be concealed in one righteous man, and the righteousness of one should justify many that are iniquitous ! Having then in the former time demonstrated the inability of our nature to obtain life, and having now revealed a saviour able to save even creatures which have no ability, he willed that for both reasons we should believe in his goodness and should regard him as nurse, father, teacher, counsellor, physician, mind, light, honour, glory, strength and life." (Epistle to Diognetus ix, trans. Lightfoot.)

It was the rediscovery of this Gospel which gave new life to the Church in the sixteenth century, and there are signs that the same thing is happening in our time. Professor Otto Piper, writing in 1934,* says : " Progressive theology emphasises that there is no really Christian experience as long as we do not believe in the justification of our whole existence through God's mercy ".

Gerhard Kittel's famous Wörterbuch is playing a leading part in this revival, bringing all the relevant resources of modern knowledge to the interpretation of Scripture. In the present volume a brief but penetrating study of Justice in the Old Testament, by Dr. Quell, and a short contribution from Dr. Kleinknecht on Greek ideas, lead to a full presentation and interpretation of Jewish and early Christian material in Dr. Schrenk's discussion of the great words of the New Testament. We are fortunate in having already in English two exceptionally good

* *Recent Developments in German Protestantism*, p. 117.

articles on Righteousness, one (O.T.) by John Skinner *
and the other (N.T.) by James Moffatt.† The present
work serves to confirm and supplement these, Dr.
Schrenk's exposition of the doctrine of Justification
being of special value. The linguistic material
has been abbreviated in this translation, but nothing
has been omitted which bears directly on the exegesis
of the New Testament.

The Greek words under consideration present
difficulties to the German translator, and further it is not
always easy to be sure of the precise English equivalents
for the terms which he uses. It is the old problem
of ben Sira's grandson, and I can only say with him that
some diligence and travail have been applied to the
matter, in the knowledge that "things originally
spoken in one language have not the same force when
they are translated into another".‡ The best intro-
duction to the pages which follow is that part of
The Bible and the Greeks (pp. 42-59), in which C. H.
Dodd treats of "righteousness", reminding us that
"the apostle [Paul] wrote Greek, and read the LXX,
but he was also familiar with the Hebrew original.
Thus while his language largely follows that of the
LXX, the Greek words are for him always coloured
by their Hebrew association."

Gottlob Schrenk was born at Frankfurt am Main
on 10th February, 1879, his father being the founder of
the "Deutsche kirkliche freie Evangelisation". He
studied theology at Erlangen, Tübingen, Halle, Bonn
and Geneva, and was specially influenced by Martin
Kähler and Adolf Schlatter. After working as a
Rhineland pastor, as Missions-inspektor in the Ostafrika-
mission at Bielefeld, and as a lecturer at the Theological

* *Hastings, D. B.* IV, 272-281.
† *Hastings Dict. Apost. Ch.* II, 370-392.   ‡ *Ecclus. Prolo ue.*

School in Bethel bei Bielefeld, he was appointed in 1923 to the Chair of New Testament at Zürich, occupying it until 1949.

A list of Dr. Schrenk's other writings is given below; * but his main literary work since 1932 has been for the " Kittel " N.T. Dictionary, and this has continued since his retirement. Among his numerous contributions are the articles on βούλομαι, γράφω, ἐντολή, εὐδοκία θέλω, ἱερός, ἐκλεκτός, λεῖμμα, and soon we are to have the longest of all, on πατήρ.

J. R. Coates.

* Gottesreich und Bund im älteren Protestantismus, vornehmlich bei Johannes Coccejus.   Zugleich ein Beitrag zur Geschichte des Pietismus und der heilsgeschichtlichen Theologie, 1923.

Grundmotive des Glaubens, 1928.

Die Geschichtsanschauung des Paulus auf dem Hintergrund seines Zeitalters, 1932. (Jahrbuch der theologischen Schule Bethel.)

Der Römerbrief als Missionsdokument, 1933. (Festgabe für E. F. K. Müller.)

Urchristliche Missionspredigt im ersten Jahrhundert, 1948. (Festgabe für Th. Wurm.)

Rabbinische Charakterköpfe im urchristlichen Zeitalter, 1945. (Judaica I, ii.)

Sabbat oder Sonntag, 1946.   (Judaica II, iii.)

Was bedeutet " Israel Gottes " Gal. vi, 16 ?   1949.   (Judaica V, ii.)

Der Segensspruch nach der Kampfesepistel : Erwiderung auf Prof. Dahl, Oslo, 1950.   (Judaica VI, iii.)

CONTENTS

ix

BIBLIOGRAPHY

W. BAUDISSIN : Kyrios III, 379-428, 1929.
H. BECK : Neue Jahrb. f. deutsche Theol. IV, 249 ff., 1895.
J. A. BEET : Expositor V, vii., 275 ff., 1898.
BOUSSET-GRESSMANN : Rel. d. Jud., 379 ff., 393.
H. BRAUN : Gerichtsged. u. Rechtfert. bei Paul, 1890.
K. BRUGMANN : Indogerm. Forsch. XXXIX, 144-149, 1921.
R. BULTMANN : R.G.G., 2nd edn., IV, 1037 f.
H. CREMER : Die paul. Rechtf. Lehre, 2nd edn., 1900.
CREMER-KÖGEL : Wörterbuch d. N.T. Gr., 1923.
J. DENNEY : Expositor IV, 4, 1901.
L. DIESTEL : Jahrb. f. deutsche Theol. V, 173 ff., 1860.
E. VON DOBSCHÜTZ : Th.St.Kr. LXXV, 38 ff., 1912.
V. EHRENBERG : Die Rechtsidee in frühen Griechentum, 1921.
K. H. FALGREN : Uppsala Dissertation on $ç^e dhaqah$, 1932.
F. V. FILSON : St. Paul's Conception of Recompense, 1931.
E. FRAENKEL : Gr. Denominativa, 68 f., 73, 124, 1906.
G. A. FRICKE : Der paul. Grundbegr. d. Δικαιοσύνη θεοῦ, 1888.
H. FUCHS : Christentum und Wissenschaft III, 101-118, 1927.
W. GRUNDMANN : Z.N.W. XXXII, 52-65, 1933.
J. H. GERRETSEN : Rechtvaardigmaking bij Paulus, 1905.
J. GONDA : Utrecht Dissertation on Δείκνυμι etc. 224-232, 1929.
Th. HAERING : Th.St.Kr. LXIX, 139 ff., 1896.
J. HEMPEL : Z.S.Th. X, 377-395, 1930.
H. W. HERTZBERG : Z.A.W. XL, 256-287, 1922.
R. HIRZEL : Themis, Dike, etc. 56-227, 1907.
W. JAEGER : Paideia, 1934.
E. KAUTZSCH : Über die Derivate d. Stammes ç$edheq$, 1881.
G. KITTEL : Th.St.Kr. LXXX, 217 ff.
P. KÖLBING : Th.St.Kr. LXVIII, 7 ff., 1895.
P. KRETSCHMER : Glotta I, 381, 1907.
E. KÜHL : Rechtfertigung, etc. bei Paulus, 1904.
K. G. KUHN : Z.N.W. XXX, 305-310, 1931.
R. A. LIPSIUS : Die paul. Rechtf. Lehre, 1853.
E. LOHMEYER : Grundlagen paulin. Theol., 1929.
W. MACHOLZ : Th.St.Kr. LXXX, 29 ff., 1915.
W. MICHAELIS : Festgabe f. A. Deissmann, 1927.
A. MICHELSEN : Z.W.L. V, 133 ff., 1884.
K. MITTRING : Heilswirklichkeit bei Paulus, 1929.
C. G. MONTEFIORE : Judaism and St. Paul, 1914.
MOULTON-MILLIGAN : Vocabulary of the Gk. Test.
E. F. K. MÜLLER : Beobachtungen z. paul. Rechtf. Lehre, 1905.

W. Mundle : Der Glaubensbegriff des Paulus, 1932.

K. Oltmanns : Th.Bl., VIII, 110-116, 1929.

C. von Orelli : Z.W.L. V, 73 ff., 1864.

R. Reitzenstein : Hell. Myst., 257 ff.

A. Ritschl : Die christl. Lehre v. d. Rechtf., etc. II, 4th edn., 1900.

A. Robertson : Expositor V, 9, 187 ff., 1899.

J. H. Ropes : J.B.L. XXII, 211 ff., 1903.

A. Schlatter : Der Glaube im N.T., 4th edn., 1927, etc.

A. Schmitt : Natalicium f. J. Geffcken, 111-131, 1931.

H. Schultz : Th.St.Kr. LXIII, 1890.

A. Schweitzer : The Mysticism of Paul the Apostle, Trans. 1931.

C. A. A. Scott : Christianity According to St. Paul, 1927.

H. St. J. Thackeray : The Relation of St. P. to cont. Jew. Thought, 1900.

Th. Thalheim : Pauly-Wissowa V, s.v. Δίκη, 1905.

E. Tobac : Le Probléme de la Justification dans St. Paul, 1908.

E. Vischer : R.G.G., 2nd edn., IV, 1745 ff.

H. E. Weber : Eschatol. u. Myst. im N.T. 90 ff., 109 ff., 1930.

G. P. Wetter : Der Vergeltungsged. bei Paulus, 161 ff., 1912.

E. Wissmann : D. Verhältnis v. πίστις u. Chr. Frömmigkeit, 1926.

O. Zänker : Z.S.Th. IX, 398-420, 1931.

[S. A. Cook : (See p. 8).

C. H. Dodd : The Bible and the Greeks, 42-59, 1935.

J. Denney, P. Shorey, and others : E.R.E. X, 777-811, 1918.

E. G. Hirsch : J.E. X, 420-424.

R. H. Kennett, Mrs. Adam, H. M. Gwatkin : Early Ideals of Righteousness 1910.

T. W. Manson : Law and Religion, ed. Rosenthal, 127 ff., 1938.

J. Moffatt : (See Preface, p. vii).

A. D. Nock : St. Paul VI, VIII and Bibliography 1938.; Conversion, 1933.

N. L. Robinson : Christian Justice, 1922.

E. Schürer : Gesch. d. Jüd. Volkes, 4th edn., II, 545-579, 1907. Cf. Eng. Tr., 92 f., 1885.

J. Skinner : (See Preface, p. vii).

C. Ryder Smith : The Bible Doctrine of Society, 125-159, 1920.]

For Paul see Commentaries on Rom. and Gal., esp. Excursus in Lietzmann, Sanday and Headlam, Zahn ; and for O.T. Theology esp. Eichrodt, [Davidson], Sellin.

Note.—Square brackets indicate additions by the translator.

ABBREVIATIONS

A.G.G.	Abhandlungen d. Kgl. Gesellschaft d. Wissensch. zu Göttingen.
A.P.F.	Archiv f. Papyrusforschung.
Bill.	Strack u. Billerbeck, Komm. z. N.T. aus Talmud u. Midrasch, 1922-8.
C.A.H.	Cambridge Ancient History.
C.B.	Cambridge Bible.
D.A.C.	Hastings Dictionary of the Apostolic Church.
E.R.E.	Hastings Encyclopædia of Religion and Ethics.
H.D.B.	Hastings Dictionary of the Bible (5 vols.).
J.B.L.	Journal of Biblical Literature (Philadelphia).
J.E.	Jewish Encyclopedia.
J.T.S.	Journal of Theological Studies.
R.G.G.	Die Religion in Geschichte und Gegenwart, 2nd edn., 1927 ff.
S.A.B.	Sitzungsberichte . . . Akademie . . . Berlin.
Th.Bl.	Theologische Blätter.
Th.St.Kr.	Theologische Studien und Kritiken.
W.A.	Weimar edition of Luther.
Z.A.W.	Zeitschr. f. A.T. Wissenschaft.
Z.S.Th.	Zeitschrift f. systematische Theologie.
Z.W.L.	Zeitschrift f. kirkliche Wissenschaft u. kirkl. Leben.

I. JUSTICE IN THE OLD TESTAMENT

ALL mutual relationships in Israel were viewed in the light of the idea of justice, and this inevitably determined theological apprehension of the relation established between God and man. The Old Testament doctrine of God is based on the idea of justice, which in turn receives ethical reinforcement through its association with religion. Linguistic usage makes this clear, a variety of expressions being used to indicate, not only the true nature of the mutual relations of God and man, but also divine and human behaviour under these conditions. The supreme importance of justice as a norm in religion gives it validity in ethics.

1. LINGUISTIC

The wealth of the Hebrew vocabulary is shown by the variety of terms for which LXX uses δίκη, δικαιοσύνη, δίκαιος, δικαιοῦν, while an examination of the different terms used throughout LXX for the principal Hebrew words shows how carefully the Greek translators tried to reproduce the sense of the original—even where their rendering is not quite happy.

Δίκη is used 9 times for *ribh* (verb and noun), but only once for *din* (Ps. ix, 5), once for *mishpaṭ* (Ps. cxl, 12 [Heb. 13] LXX cxxxix, 13) and once for the obscure *haruç* (Joel iii, 14–Heb. and LXX iv, 14, " decision " ?). As a rendering of *naqam* (Exod. xxi, 20 ; Lev. xxvi, 25 ; Deut. xxxii, 41, 43), it weakens the idea of vengeance. Its use at Hos. xiii, 14, seems to be a mistake due to the confusion

of *debher* with *dabhar*. It is surprising that LXX is
so sparing in the use of δίκη ; one would have expected it frequently as an accurate rendering of
mishpaṭ or even *çedheq*.

Δικαιοσύνη occurs relevantly for *çedheq* 81 times,
for *çᵉdhaqah* 134 times, and in periphrasis for *çaddiq* 6
times (Ps. lxxii, 7–LXX lxxi, 7 ; Prov. ii, 20 ; xi, 21,
30 ; xv, 6 ; xx, 7) ; cf. also Is. xxvi, 2. Its equivalent is *ḥeṣedh* only 8 times (Gen. xix, 19 ; xx, 13 ; xxi,
23 ; xxxii, 10 ; Exod. xv, 13 ; xxxiv, 7 ; Prov. xx,
28–LXX 22 ; Is. lxiii, 7), and *'ᵉmeth* 6 times (Gen.
xxiv, 49 ; Josh. xxiv, 14 ; Is. xxxviii, 19 ; xxxix, 8 ;
Dan. viii, 12 ; ix, 13). It is also used for *mesharim*
(I Chron. xxix, 17) ; *ṭobh* (Ps. xxxviii, 21–LXX
xxxvii, 21) ; *madhon* (Prov. xvii, 14) ; *niqqayon* (Gen.
xx, 5) ; even for *pethi*, " simplicity " (Prov. i, 22) and
zakhu (Aram.), " innocence " (Dan. vi, 23, [but cf.
Heb. *zakhah*, Micah vi, 11 ; Ps. li, 6]). Through
carelessness it stands for *haskel* at Prov. xxi, 16.

Δίκαιος occurs 189 times for *çaddiq* ; in free rendering 24 times for *çedheq* ; 5 times for *çᵉdhaqah* ; at
Dan. xii, 3 for *hiçdiq*. It is also found for *yashar*
(Job i, 1, 8 ; ii, 3 ; Prov. iii, 32 ; xi, 4 ; xiv, 9 ;
xxi, 2, 18) ; *naqi* (Job. ix, 23 ; xvii, 8, etc.) ; *tamim*
(Prov. xxviii, 18). Elsewhere it is used loosely for
'ᵉmeth, *din*, *ḥeṣedh*, *ṭahor*, *mishpaṭ*, *nadhibh* and *naqam*.

Δικαιοῦν comes relevantly 21 times for various parts
of the verb *çadhaq*, and once for the noun *çedheq*
(Is. xlii, 21) ; twice for *ribh* (Mic. vii, 9 and Is. i, 17) ;
once for *shaphaṭ* (Niph. at I Sam. xii, 7) ; and a few
times for parts of *zakhah* and *baḥan*.

Δικαίωμα stands for *ḥoq* (48 times), *ḥuqqah* (22),
mishpaṭ (38), *miçwah* (Deut. xxx, 16 ; I Kings ii, 3),
çᵉdhaqah (II Sam. xix, 28 ; Prov. viii, 20), *ribh* (Jer.
xi, 20 ; xviii, 19) and, with less appropriateness, a
few other terms.

The one Hebrew expression which is generally represented by δίκη and its derivatives (esp. δικαιοσύνη) is *çedheq* and its derivatives, other synonymous terms being very rarely thus indicated. Of the latter, *mishpaṭ* stands out as a word not sufficiently appreciated by LXX; its connotation in Hebrew is only partly conveyed by LXX κρίμα (182 times) and κρίσις (142), which emphasise the act of judgment. Another word for which δικαιοσύνη is an excellent equivalent is *ḥesedh*: but LXX prefers to use ἔλεος (172 times), emphasising the emotional element without due regard to Hebrew usage. The Greek translators also failed to appreciate the value of *tamam* and its derivatives in the sphere of *çᵉdhaqah* and *mishpaṭ*.

Our key words are thus *mishpaṭ*,[1] *çedheq* (*çᵉdhaqah*),[2] *ḥesedh*,[3] and *ḥoq*.[4] These terms, like *bᵉrith*, have both

---

[1] *Mishpaṭ* exemplifies almost all the types of meaning which belong to nouns with the prefix *M*. The primary sense of "judgment", concrete (I Kings xx, 40 : Ps. xvii, 2) or more abstract (Lev. xix, 15), gives rise to its common use for legal norm, legal claim, legal custom.

[2] There seems to be no difference in meaning between the masculine and feminine forms. The shorter form is preferred for the *genetivus epexegeticus*, and means "correctness".

[3] *Ḥesedh* is the natural sense of justice which regulates non-legal relationships, e.g. among members of the same tribe or group. "Love" is a misleading translation because it is always a matter of intention, having regard to what is just, and not a spontaneous, personal feeling, like *'ahebh*, etc. Love may, or may not, find expression in *ḥesedh*, which is always governed by objective considerations. A better translation, though not quite adequate, is "loyalty". (It has the late Hebrew meaning, "charm" or "grace", in Is. xl, 6, but is a scribal error, cf. I Pet. i, 24.) The etymology is obscure; cf. Nöldeke, Neue Beiträge zur sem. Sprachwiss. (1910) 93. It belongs to the covenant circle of ideas: cf. I Sam. xx, 8, etc.

[4] *Ḥoq* means something engraved or inscribed on a hard substance, and so denotes statute or law in a narrower sense.

a juristic and a theological use, and the obvious pre-
sumption that the latter grew out of the former,
though not directly demonstrable, may be allowed
to pass, since we are mainly concerned here with
theology, i.e. with the application of the words to
God or to a specifically religious attitude on the part
of man.

2. THE RIGHTEOUSNESS OF GOD

God is the author of justice, and, as a just God, is
bound to act justly ; this is the immovable ground of
Old Testament faith in all its varieties, the common
denominator which gives religious unity to Israel :
prophets, priests, lawgivers, the common people—all
are convinced of the justice of God as the disposer
of all things and the ground of hope.   It cannot be
denied that there is a causal connexion between this
association of justice with religion and the historical
development of the Yahwe religion out of a tribal
religion in which the Godhead was not only over his
people but also in fellowship with them.   Yahwe is
the fountain of justice from which all O.T. codes of
law are derived ; [1] his decisions on matters of civil
law and on political questions in the nomadic period
are made known through the sacred lot (Exod.
xxviii, 30) ; these judgments (*mishpaṭim*) form his
torah (instruction, guidance, *weisung* : Deut. xxxiii,
10).   Because he is the supreme judge, his divine
authority is involved in the details of Israel's historical
situation.   " Shall not the judge of all the earth do
right ? " (Gen. xviii, 25 J).   Abraham's trustful question may sound like an example of man's audacious

[1] " The judgment is God's " (Deut. i, 17). This is fundamental in other Semitic religions ; cf. Baudissin, Kyrios III
(1929), 382 ff.

effort to drag God into the service of his moral convictions ; but it is really an expression of absolute assurance that whatever God does must have the force of a *mishpaṭ*, and testifies to the submission that always characterises the worshippers of Yahwe. Yahwe's law is indisputable and unchangeable ; to disregard it is contrary to nature (Jer. viii, 7). " His work is perfect " (Deut. xxxii, 4)—a faultless whole, inherently permanent ; " for all his ways are judgment "—awarding to every man that which belongs to him and giving him security. Yahwe's judgment is righteous because he is righteous—" a God of faithfulness and without iniquity, just and right is he "—and as such he can be trusted ; there is nothing crooked or deceptive in his ordinance, for his thoughts are straight and true.[1]

Utterances like the one just quoted picture Yahwe as a ruler and judge discharging the duties of his office, " a righteous judge " (Ps. vii, 12 ; cf. Jer. xii, 1). This view appeared early in Israel, even when it had nothing in common with the just administration of civil law. The Song of Deborah calls the victory of the tribes of Israel " the righteous acts of Yahwe " (Judg. v, 11). It is easy to see how confidence in the judicial qualities of Yahwe leads to progress in the idea of God : if his favour is felt to be a righteous judgment in the case of a victory over nations with other gods, that must involve some sort of belief in the extension of his sovereignty over those nations. At all events it was from legal proceedings that Israel drew its picture of the world order. The danger of this view lies obviously in the fact that it postulates a splitting up of mankind into hostile groups, and leads only too easily to the forestalling

[1] Cf. Ps. xi, 7, where " righteousness " may mean either right verdicts or right actions.

of the divine judgment. Those who pray are apt to make a claim upon Yahwe's righteousness, and to ask him to pronounce their enemies guilty (e.g. Ps. v, 10, 12–Heb. 9, 11).[1] The idea of righteousness loses its objective power when the suppliant urges his own sense of justice upon the judge. God's righteousness may even come to be thought of as concerned only with the affairs of the upright and the pure (Ps. xviii, 25 f.–Heb. 26 f.). It is, however, hardly fair to such utterances, simply to track down the consequences of their theory of justice. They show, rather, how strong religious motifs can come to life out of a theologically coloured way of regarding the justice of God, so that it is hardly possible any longer to base an adequate interpretation of the application of the idea of righteousness to God upon its formal outlines alone. This belongs to the sphere of faith, for it is the expression of unconditional trust in the moral will of God, by the force of which goodness is rewarded with preservation while wickedness is condemned to destruction. Out of *çᵉdhaqah* as the norm for perfect *shalom* there develops *çᵉdhaqah* as action which achieves, renews and secures it.

3. THE RIGHTEOUSNESS OF MAN

What has just been said applies not only to divine activities, but also to human behaviour towards both God and man. Old Testament writers show a marked preference for a juristic view of ethical and religious practice. They constantly see the "righteous" pleading his cause before the judge, defending himself against malevolence and falsehood, and

---

[1] Habakkuk adapts the individual lamentation motif to the contrast between Israel and the Chaldeans, e.g. i, 13 ; cf. ii, 4.

winning his case.   In this way the good man's misery
and anxiety disappears before the mighty power of
faith in the unchangeable grace and favour of the
covenant God.   The "righteous" (*çaddiq*) is the man
whom God's verdict has justified (*hiçdiq*), and the
"wicked" (*rasha'*) is the man whom God has condemned ;   the background being the picture of a
judicial process (*ribh*).[1]   So *çaddiq* comes to mean
"godly", and *ç^edhaqah* "godliness"—as that which
earns the divine acquittal.[2]   Another term for the
latter is *'^emunah*, fidelity in the fulfilment of God's
commandments in the midst of uncertainty and
opposition.   "The righteous lives by his fidelity"
(Hab. ii, 4) :   i.e. he escapes the death penalty,
planned for him by his enemies, through his un-
flinching faithfulness to God's commandment.[3]   The
word *'^emunah* aptly expresses that which is demanded
by faith in God's righteousness and hope of his
approval.

Personal or national misfortune often enough suggests
that Yahwe's verdict is unfavourable.   In such a case
çedheq, in the sense of success,[4] is not in view ;   the
idea of "righteousness" gives place to other motifs.
Yahwe is a rock, the last refuge of the godly in dis-
tress : Ps. lxii, 7 (8), etc.   Yet even then faith can
cry,   "Unto thee, O Lord, belongeth the love of
justice (*ḥesedh*) :   for thou renderest to every man
according to his work" :   Ps. lxii, 12 (13).   Job's

[1] Cf. Deut. xxv, 1.

[2] Cf. I Sam. xxvi, 23 ; I Kings viii, 32 ; Deut. vi, 25 (here
righteousness almost means acquittal, cf. Gen. xv, 1).

[3] Paul is not mistaken in his use of the quotation in Rom. i, 17 ;
Gal. iii, 11, though he certainly reads more into the word *'^emunah*
than was intended by Habakkuk.   LXX ἐκ πίστεώς μου is most
simply explained as a mistake ; but it might be that the translator was theologising—like Paul.

[4] As of Cyrus, in Is. xli, 2 [see Skinner, C. B. (1929) *ad loc.*].

torment is the agony of doubting the righteousness of God. Is Justice between God and man really valid as a self-evident axiom? This is the question which the poet is asking in his dialogue. He knows that the traditional dogma will become a merely fantastic assertion, unless it is projected into a higher sphere.

[*Note.*—There is an important discussion, with useful references, bearing on the questions raised in chapters I and II, by S. A. Cook in W. R. Smith, *The Religion of the Semites*, 3rd ed. (1927), pp. 655-671. Cf. W. R. Smith, *The Prophets of Israel*, 2nd ed. (1902), pp. 70 ff., and S. A. Cook, *Cambridge Ancient History*, vol. II (1931), pp. 397 ff., 669 f.]

II. THE GREEK IDEA OF JUSTICE

1. GREEK society from the eighth to the beginning of the fifth century B.C. was based on the idea of justice—religious, political and ethical—and the political philosophy of the fourth century was built on the same foundation.[1] It is significant that for the Greeks it was not the rational and logical conception which came first, but the mythical figure of the goddess: " There is virgin Justice, the daughter of Zeus, who is honoured and reverenced among the gods who dwell on Olympus " (Hesiod, Works and Days, 256 f., trans. H. G. Evelyn–White).[2] Hesiod's incipient rationalism turned the sturdy figure of the goddess, sitting beside the judgment-seat of Zeus, into the reign of law, no less divine, prevailing in the world and in the life of the city, as understood by Solon.[3] Justice is for the latter still divine, although his more modern conception of divinity differs from that of Hesiod ; it is not a human device, but a law, independent of man, which he cannot evade, however he may twist and turn. The recognition of justice in politics now leads to its discovery, by analogy, as the law of the universe : the only remaining fragment

---

[1] See pp. 26 f.

[2] ἡ δέ τε παρθένος ἐστὶ Δίκη, Διὸς ἐκγεγαυῖα κυδρή τ' αἰδοίη τε θεοῖς, οἳ Ὄλυμπον ἔχουσιν. [P. Shorey, in E.R.E. (1918) X, 801, regards this as " conscious allegory " ; and it may be noted that δίκη occurs 9 times in lines 248-273, and has to be translated into 4 different English words.]

[3] Frag. i, 8 (i, 17 Diehl) ; Frag. iii, 14 ff. (i, 23 Diehl). Cf. W. Jaeger, Solons Eunomie, S.A.B. (1926), 69-85.

of Anaximander speaks of its immanence.[1] The advance from punishment by an external deity to immanent punitive justice thus leads to the conception of a divine world-order : [2] as Heraclitus has it, " For the sun will not pass his bounds, else will the avenging deities, helpers of justice, find him out " (Frag. 94, Diels I, 96).

2. Next to Solon, the greatest exponent of the idea of justice is Theognis, among whose sayings the famous verse occurs : " In justice all virtue is comprehended." [3] Justice is here, in this early period, not an inner quality, but the legally prescribed behaviour of the citizen towards society. This explains how all virtues came to be included in the later conception of δικαιοσύνη.[4] When Plato makes this the guiding principle, both for the State and for the individual (Rep. IV, 443c ff.), he is harking back to the primitive religious aspect of justice. Aristotle devotes a whole book of his treatise on ethics to δικαιοσύνη, and gives it the place of honour among the virtues (Eth. Nic. V, iii, 1129b, 27) ; it means the performance of all one's social duties (ib. v, 1130b, 11 f.). The comprehensive connotation is primary, and is to be distinguished from the narrower, juristic

[1] Frag. ix (i, 15 Diels) : the elements " make reparation and satisfaction to one another for their injustice " (δίκην καὶ τίσιν ἀλλήλοις τῆς ἀδικίας). The time-process itself continually redresses the balance. Parmenides also presents δίκη as a principle universally at work, identical with necessity or fate (Frag. viii, 12 f. ; cf. the same in Euripides—see W. Nestle, Gr. Religiosität II, 1933, 124).

[2] Cf. Jaeger, Paideia 217 ff. ; " The recognition of this law or norm in nature has a direct religious significance. It is not simply a description of fact ; it is a justification of the universe " (219).

[3] ἐν δὲ δικαιοσύνῃ συλλήβδην πᾶσ' ἀρετή ἐστιν (147, i, 124 Diehl). [Quoted from Phocylides, Frag. 15 ; see P. Shorey in E.R.E. X, 802.]   [4] See pp. 26 f.

use, which makes it one among other virtues (ib. iv, 1130*a*, 14; 1130*b*, 3 ff., 30 ff.). The double reference is also indicated by etymological research.[1]

3. Many views have been held concerning the original connotation of the word δίκη [which we have translated as "justice"]. It used to be thought, from its connexion with δείκνυμι, "indicate", that it meant "way" or "custom", as that which is indicated, and that it thus came to mean "right" or "justice".[2] Another view was that the legal reference came first, connecting it with δικεῖν, as if this meant "to strike", the reference being to the stroke of the judge's staff;[3] but this will not do, because δικεῖν means "to throw"; nor is it satisfactory to make it refer to the "throw" which determined the divine judgment.[4] Even if we connect δικεῖν with δεικνύναι[5] or take it to mean the stretching out of the hand by Justice when she makes her award,[6] this recognises as primitive only the ideas of right and justice. The fact is that from the beginning, as far as our observation extends, δίκη is used to express both sets of ideas, viz. custom, etc. as well as right, etc. The question therefore arises whether both meanings may not have been developed simultaneously from the same root; and this has now been shown to have been the case.[7]

The fundamental meaning of the root "deik" is "showing the way", "determining". It is represented figuratively by the outstretched hand. Δίκη

---

[1] Paragraphs 1 and 2 are contributed by Hermann Kleinknecht.

[2] G. Curtius, Grundzüge der Gr. Etymol., 5th ed. (1879), 134; Cremer-Kögel, 296. Gonda (see Bibl.), 216 f. Aristotle's derivation from δίχα is only valuable for the appended comment (Eth. Nic. V, vii, 1132*a*, 28).

[3] Hirzel, 60 ff., 94. [Cf. E.R.E. X, 801.]

[4] Ehrenberg, 76 ff.   [5] Brugmann, 144 ff.

[6] Kretschmer, 268.   [7] Gonda, 228, 230 f.

thus means directing, determining, and that which is directed or determined (cf. statuere, statutum, etc.). This is the starting-point for both lines of development, which may be traced as follows.

General. (*a*) What is usual : Homer, Od. iv, 691 ; what is right : Pindar, Ol. ii, 18 ; manner : Pindar, Pyth. ii, 84 ; traditional custom : II Macc. viii, 26 (A), and frequently in the Papyri. (*b*) Due : Hesiod, Shield of H., 85 ; fair dealing : Homer, Od. xiv, 84 ; reciprocity (cf. Aristot. Eth. Nic. V, vii, 1131*b*). (*c*) Fate, natural necessity,[1] lot : Homer, Od. xi, 218 ; the corresponding Sanskrit root means " lot ".

Juristic. (*a*) Justice : Homer, Il. xvi, 388 ; in Hesiod (see p. 9) it means the right of the oppressed, recognised by the community ;[2] Josephus, War, V, 2. (*b*) Legal action, judgment : Homer and Hesiod ; LXX for *ribh,* Job xxix, 16 ; *din,* Ps. ix, 4 (5) ; *mishpat,* Ps. cxl, 12 (13) ; *haruç,* Joel iii, 14 ; also Josephus, Philo, Epictetus. (*c*) Punishment, commonly personified[3] (cf. Wis. xi, 20), but also impersonally, esp. in LXX, e.g. Exod. xxi, 20.[4]

4. The New Testament has δίκη only 3 times, viz., Acts xxviii, 4 ; II Thess. i, 9 ; Jude 7 ; always in the sense of punishment or penal justice. (The true reading in Acts xxv, 15, is καταδίκην, condemnation.)

---

[1] Ehrenberg, 60.   [2] Ehrenberg, 65 f.

[3] Schlatter (Theol. Jud., 40 ff.) rightly emphasises the personification of δίκη by Josephus : e.g. Bell. vii, 34. At IV Macc. viii, 14, 22 δίκη is merciful.

[4] On δίκη in Corp. Herm. cf. J. Kroll, Die Lehren des Herm. Trismeg. (1914) 219 f.

III. RIGHTEOUS

I. GREEK AND HELLENISTIC

(a) Δίκαιος denotes one who is correct according to the traditions of polite society, observing δίκη as opposed to ὕβρις (Homer, Od. vi, 119 ff.).

(b) It also covers duty towards man and towards God. Usually the latter is expressed by ὅσιος, εὐσεβής, θεοφιλής, θεοσεβής; δίκαιος being frequently used with one of these to indicate one who does both his moral and his religious duty, e.g. Jos. Ant., x, 215.[1] An example of the purely religious reference is Aesch. Seven ag. Th., 594, where it is contrasted with δυσσεβής.

(c) A specially common use of δίκαιος is for one who observes legal norms; as Aristotle says, " Clearly the righteous man will be he who is both law-abiding and impartial " (Eth. Nic. V, ii, 1129a, 33).

(d) Moral philosophy extends the reference of the term so as to embrace the whole of life, with all its social virtues, making what is righteous equivalent to what is beautiful, good, fitting (Epict. Diss., I, xxii, 1 ; II, xvii, 6). The quality indicated by δίκαιος thus takes its place as one of the four cardinal virtues, wisdom, temperance, justice, courage.[2] The Stoic

[1] Schlatter op. cit. 37, points out that Josephus here expresses a Pharisaic idea, similar to Jesus' summary of the Law as love to God and man. As a Hellenistic Jew, he is debtor both to Greece and to the O.T. ; but though his idiom is Greek, he knows well that for the Jew religion is everything (Ap. ii, 171, 181).

[2] The fourfold summary of virtues is considerably older than Plato, being found first in Aeschylus (Sept. c. Theb. 610). Wilamowitz wrongly regarded the line as an interpolation from a Platonic source. Aeschylus was no doubt using an early Greek idea.

interpretation makes it specially clear that man is here always considered theoretically and never empirically. And indeed Plato himself, though expressly treating of justice as a political virtue, finds the root of the matter in the human soul, where the individual is truly himself, with all his powers in order and harmony (Rep. iv, 433c ff.). Δίκαιος thus comes to signify an innate quality of human nature, of which man avails himself in his activities.[1] Josephus not only regards it as belonging to the sphere of virtue, but goes the length of speaking of his heroes as men who are "naturally" (τὴν φύσιν) righteous, e.g. Ant. vii, 110 ; ix, 216, etc., and calls the opposite of righteousness a deviation from virtue (Ant. vi, 93) ; his δίκαιος may refer either to virtue or to faithfulness to the Law, but his lists of virtues always include righteousness along with goodness, etc., and differ in no way from those of his non-Jewish contemporaries, e.g. Ant. ix, 260.[2]

Philo is still more pronounced in his emphasis on righteousness as one of the cardinal virtues. His excessive praise of the righteous is suggestive of the Hellenistic glorification of man. As the mainstay of the human race, the righteous man stands over against the unrighteous multitude, exercising the healing influence of the justice which has made him whole (Migr. Abr. 61, 121, 124 ; Det. Pot. Ins. 123) ; he seeks the essential nature of things (Leg. All. III, 78). Faith is a δίκαιον, i.e. a meritorious virtue (Rer. Div.

---

[1] ["This cheerful acceptance of man's nature as being disposed to walk aright, provided that his powers and instincts are duly guided, and not warped by hardships or excessive prosperity, runs throughout the whole course of Greek thought" (Mrs. Adam in Early Ideals of Righteousness, 1910, p. 35).]

[2] Josephus is fond of associating δίκαιος with words for goodness, such as εὔνοια (Ant. i, 318), ἀγαθός (vii, 389 ; viii, 248) or χρηστός (ix, 133).

Her. 94), displayed in the patriarchs—specially in Noah, on the ground of a mistaken etymology—who are called righteous on this account (Leg. All. III, 228 ; Det. Pot. Ins. 121). This is, of course, a blending of Hellenistic ethics with the Old Testament description of the godly man as " the righteous " (ςaddiq). Apart from the points mentioned, Josephus and Philo keep close to Hebrew and Jewish tradition. Josephus is familiar with the Pharisaic conception of righteousness as obedience to God's commandments (Ap. ii, 293, etc.), uses δίκαιος in the sense of " punctilious " (Ant. xv, 106), and holds the conviction that righteousness can be gained through repentance (Ant. vi, 21). Philo applies δίκαιος to God much more frequently than Josephus, e.g. Somn. II, 194.

(e) A quantitative view of morality is indicated by the frequent appearance of the comparative and superlative of δίκαιος in Greek writers of all ages, but these are not found in the New Testament.

(f) The application of δίκαιος to things is also absent from the N.T., though it is used with "judgment" (John v, 30 ; [cf. Rev. xvi, 7 ; xix, 2]) ; "ways" (Rev. xv, 3) ; [" commandment " (Rom. vii, 12)]. " Righteous blood " (Matt. xxiii, 35) means "innocent ", cf. xxvii, 4, and Jonah i, 14, LXX.

(g) Tὸ δίκαιον is defined by Aristotle as "that which is legal and fair " (Eth. Nic. V, ii, 1129a, 34 : τὸ μὲν δίκαιον ἄρα τὸ νόμιμον καὶ τὸ ἴσον, τὸ δ' ἄ δικον τὸ παράνομον καὶ τὸ ἄνισον) ; cf. Col. iv, 1. Other definitions reflect different ideals of justice,[1] the Pythagoreans equating it with retaliation, Plato with the virtue of the citizen who obeys the law of his own nature.[2] The Plural (τά δίκαια) is used in a juristic sense, esp. in the Papyri, meaning rights, orders, claims, etc. LXX has both Sing. and Plur. in this

[1] Hirzel 186 ff.　　　[2] See p. 14.

sense,[1] but it is not found in the N.T. Josephus applies the term δίκαιον to all law, Jewish and Gentile, and can speak of "natural right" (War I, 507 : τὸ τῆς φύσεως δίκαιον).

(h) Josephus also uses δίκαιος with verbs of thinking (cf. II Pet. i, 13), speaking, doing, etc., as the N.T. uses δικαιοσύνη (Matt. vi, 1 ; Rom. ix, 30). The latter word with him refers to the practice of right, the former to its content.

(i) The simple conventional formula, "it is right", occurs in Josephus, sometimes meaning "according to the Law".

(j) The adverb means "with full right" or "deservedly" or "justly", and is used with the verb "judge" (Deut. i, 16 ; Prov. xxxi, 9 (LXX xxiv, 77) ; Ecclus. xxxii, 22), and with "suffer" (Wis. xix, 13 ; Test. Sim. iv, 3).

2. SEPTUAGINT

A decisive change in the use of δίκαιος took place in the LXX, in spite of what has been said about its conformity with ordinary Greek and Hellenistic usage, under the influence of O.T. faith, which had the effect of linking it closely with the thought of the judgment of God. The idea of virtue gave place to the fundamental question of man's standing in the light of that judgment, as made known in the Law. The rest of Greek literature means by δίκαιος one who does what is commonly thought to be right, fulfilling his duty as a citizen ; here it means one who obeys God as a member of the theocratic community. This comes out very clearly in the words used to indicate the opposite of δίκαιος, viz. ἄδικος, Prov. xii, 17 ; xxix, 27 ; ἁμαρτωλός, Ps. cxxv, 3 (LXX

---

[1] E.g. Job viii, 3 ; xxxiv, 12, A ; Prov. xvi, 33 ; xviii, 5.

cxxiv, 3) ; Tob. iv, 17 ; ἀσεβής, Gen. xviii, 23 ;
Prov. x, 28 ; Wis. iii, 10 ; παράνομος, Job. xvii, 8.

The background of this is the conviction that God
himself is δίκαιος. Hellenistic Judaism thus pre-
pares the way for the central religious value of the
term in the New Testament, by maintaining that
God always observes the self-imposed law of his own
being, and never fails to fulfil his promises, in loyalty
to his covenant : e.g. I Sam. ii, 2 [not in Heb.] ;
Ezra ix, 15 ; Tob. iii, 2. God is said to be just and
holy (δίκαιος καὶ ὅσιος) : Deut. xxxii, 4 ; Ps. cxlv
(cxliv), 17. It is not only as the righteous judge,
inflicting just punishment, that God is called δίκαιος,
but also as the bestower of salvation : Ps. cxvi (cxiv), 5
(see p. 30).

3. RABBINICAL JUDAISM

(a) The doctrine of rewards and punishments led
the Rabbis to draw a hard and fast line between the
righteous and the godless, and to take an optimistic
view of man's ability to achieve righteousness before
God. Corresponding to δίκαιος are the Hebrew
çaddiq, yashar, kasher, and their Aramaic equivalents,[1]
which mean that a man has observed the Law
generally,[2] and that his merits outweigh his transgressions. The godless man is he whose balance is
on the other side. Two further types are also recognised, viz. the mediocre (benoni)[3] and the penitent
(ba'al t^eshubhah).[4] Hillel and Shammai differed in
their views of the former,[5] and there was keen debate

[1] çaddiqa', koshra', kashshira', zakka'ah, zakka'y. See Billerbeck
III, 222 f.
[2] Bab. Ab. Z. 4a ; Shir Rabb. ii, 1 (62a), etc. ; see Bill. I, 816.
[3] Jer. R. ha Sh. 57a, 49, Bill. III, 230 f.
[4] Bab. Sukkah 53a Bar., Bill. II, 211.
[5] Bill. II, 361 f.

as to whether the penitent or the perfectly righteous
should be given the highest place.[1] The patriarchs
were accounted perfectly righteous, partly because
they perfectly repressed the evil inclination.[2] The
striking prominence of Abel in the N.T. has no parallel
in Rabbinical literature, which never tires of pointing
to Abraham, Isaac, Jacob [3] and others,[4] while Philo
refers to Noah.[5] (On the merit of the Fathers, cf.
p. 32 [and see M. Joseph in E.R.E. xi, 144 f.]).

Many teachers are specially commended as being
righteous, and the prophet and the righteous often
go together.[6] The prayer of a righteous man,
towards whom God's heart goes out,[7] changes severity
into mercy.[8]

(b) The Messiah is called righteous, because he is
altogether conformed to the divine will. Both Rabbis
and apocalyptic writers frequently use the predicate
in this connexion.[9] The synagogue loves the expression, " Messiah our righteousness ",[10] with special

[1] Bab. Ber. 34b, Bill. I, 603.

[2] Bab. B.B. 16b-17a Bar., Bill. III, 187 ; IV, 479.

[3] Cf. Prayer Man. 8.

[4] Cf. Schlatter, Matt. 688.

[5] Cf. Ecclus. xliv, 17.

[6] Pesiqta Rab. 40 (167b), Bill. III, 124.

[7] Bab. Yeb. 64a, Bab. Ḥull. 60b, Bill. I, 453.

[8] Bab. Sukkah 14a, Bill. I, 454. On the prayer of the
righteous, see Enoch xlvii, 1, 4 ; xcvii, 3, 4 ; Jos. Bell. v, 403.
[Cf. Prov. xv, 8, 29 ; James v, 16.]

[9] H. Dechent, Der " Gerechte "—eine Bezeichnung für den
Messias, Theol. Stud. Krit. 100 (1927-1928), 439 ff. Cf. as
parallels the δίκαιον πνεῦμα of Apollo (Anc. Gr. Inscr. Brit.
Mus. IV, 1062) and δίκαιος as epithet of Isis, P. Roussel, Les
Cultes Egyptiens à Delos (1925 f.), 171, 276.

[10] Pesiqta Rab. 36 (162a) ; 37 (162b, 163a), Billerbeck II,
289 f. Cf. Shemoneh 'Esreh 14 (Palest. Rec.) : Meshiaḥ çidhqekha,
thy righteous Messiah, Bill. IV, 213 [text in Dalman, Die Worte
Jesu (1898), 300].

reference to Jer. xxiii, 5 [1] and 6 [2] ; xxxiii, 15 [3] ; Zech.
ix, 9.[4] On the other hand Is. liii, 11*b* and Dan.
xii, 3, are taken to mean Israel and those who are
righteous.[5] Only since the third century A.D. has
Is. liii, 11 been interpreted Messianically.[6] The book
of Wisdom abounds in the use of the title "the
Righteous" for the Messiah, e.g. at ii, 18.[7] The
Psalms of Solomon also associate righteousness with
the Messiah : xvii, 25, 28, 31, 35, 42 ; xviii, 8 f. It
is fundamental in Enoch (xxxviii, 2 ; liii, 6) that
righteousness is the characteristic of the Messianic
age, and the righteous will obtain the greatest promises
in the day of salvation, because of their good works.[8]
At Habakkuk ii, 4 faithfulness is the summing-up of
a life of meritorious obedience to the Law.[9]

4. NEW TESTAMENT

A deep gulf separates the N.T. δίκαιος from the
world of Greek idealism, in which every man is the
captain of his own soul. Echoes of the latter are
heard in the Gospels, e.g. when Romans apply the
conventional epithet to Jesus ; and the word is also

[1] Targ., Bill. II, 113.

[2] Bab. Bab. B. 75*b* ; Shir Rabb. on i, 16, Bill. I, 66 ; Midr.
Ps. xxi, § 2, ib. II, 352 ; Midr. Prov. xix, 21, ib. IV, 784.

[3] Targ., Bill. II, 113.

[4] Pes. Rab. 34 (159*b*), Bill. I, 844.

[5] Bill. I, 481-485. [6] Bab. Sanh. 98*b*, ib. 481 f.

[7] [But cf. R. H. Charles, Eschatology 2nd ed. (1913) 309 :
"Our author makes no reference to the Messiah" ; J. A. F.
Gregg, C.B. (1909) xlviii : "Strictly speaking, there is no
Messianic hope in Wisdom" ; E. Schürer, Gesch. Jüd. Volk.,
4th ed. (1907) II, 593 : "The former Messianic interpretation
of Wis. ii, 12-20 is totally unfounded."]

[8] Bill. IV, 799 ff.

[9] Targ., Hab. ii, 4, Bill. III, 542 ; cf. ib. I, 907.

3

found in some common phrases which are not bound
up with the Greek view of life. Otherwise this term
provides a specially good example of the influence of
the Old Testament and of the change brought about
by the Gospel.

(a) When Pilate's wife calls Jesus righteous (Matt.
xxvii, 19), she may mean both that he is innocent
and that he is a good man from the ethical point of
view, unless she—or the narrator—is "judaising".[1]
The same can be said of the use of the word by Pilate
himself (Matt. xxvii, 24).[2] The centurion at the
Cross (Luke xxiii, 47), and Herod, speaking of John
the Baptist (Mark vi, 20), are to be understood as
meaning what is commonly meant when a man is
called a saint, the former indicating innocence as
well. Paul includes " whatsoever things are just " in
the list of social virtues which he borrows from
Hellenism (Phil. iv, 8), but it is inconceivable that he
should mean anything other than doing God's will.
Another clear echo of Greek ethics is heard in the
language of Titus ii, 12, but there is nothing Greek
in the thought of the passage.

We need not dwell on the use of δίκαιον, etc., in
common phrases, e.g. II Pet. i, 13 ; Luke xii, 57 ;
Col. iv, 1 ; Matt. xx, 4 ; Phil. i, 7 ; but in some
cases it has been found necessary to deepen the meaning by adding an explicit reference to God : e.g.
Acts iv, 19 ; II Thess. i, 6 ; and of course this reference
is implied in Eph. vi, 1 (cf. Josephus Ant. ix, 58).

(b) The connotation of δίκαιος in the New Testament is largely determined by the Old Testament ;

---

[1] Acta Pilati, 2nd ed. 1876 (Tischendorf), 223.
[2] τοῦ δικαίου is not in B D Syr. Sin. On the other hand, the
apostles are called οἱ δίκαιοι in the Harkleian margin at Acts
xiv, 2.

but a new feature comes into view, which may be illustrated as follows.

(i) In line with the O.T. are passages which speak of God as Judge, e.g. Rev. xv, 3 ; xvi, 5, 7 ; xix, 2 ; I Pet. ii, 23 ; John xvii, 25. As these confirm and deepen the idea of the divine justice, so Rom. vii, 12 emphasises the truth that the Law is invested with the glory of its Author.

On the other hand, it is something new, when absolute justice is said to be shown in the atonement through the sacrificial death of Jesus (Rom. iii, 26) and when God is called "faithful and just to forgive our sins" (I John i, 9), δίκαιος combining the ideas of judgment and salvation. In both these examples the influence of Is. xl-lv and Psalms can be recognised ; what is new is the linking of righteousness with the atoning death of Christ, in which God is proved to be δίκαιος.

(ii) As applied to the Messiah, δίκαιος has its O.T. meaning at Acts iii, 13 f. and vii, 52, and refers to the perfect obedience of Jesus to the will of God, the context also suggesting his innocence in contrast to those who put him to death, in line with the preaching of the Cross in Acts (cf. Matt. xxvii, 4, where some MSS have δίκαιον). The attestation of the innocent victim in the resurrection is meant at Acts xxii, 14. Those who belong to the righteous Jesus must do righteousness, in opposition to licentiousness (I John ii, 29 ; iii, 7).[1] Christ's vicarious death is presented in I Pet. iii, 18 as the suffering of the righteous for the unrighteous. According to I John ii, 1 he continues his vicarious work in the sphere of glory.

[1] Both passages are in amplification of what Bultmann calls "Homileten" (Analyse des I Joh., Festg. f. A. Jülicher, 1927, 138-158).

In all these cases the righteous Christ does the will of
God to perfection.

On the other hand, John v, 30 represents Christ
as sharing in the righteous judgment of God at the
end of the world, for the (typically Johannine) reason
that he is completely devoted to the will of God,
and this is contrasted with judging according to
appearance (vii, 24). Cf. II Tim. iv, 8.

(iii) Men who do God's will are called righteous, as
in the O.T. : e.g. Abel (Matt. xxiii, 35 ; Heb. i, 14 ;
cf. I John iii, 12) and Lot (II Pet. ii, 7 f.), in contrast
with their lawless neighbours. With such examples
are coupled the prophet and the martyr (Matt.
xiii, 17 ; xxiii, 29, 35 ; cf. [v, 10-12 ;] x, 41). See
also Luke i, 6 ; ii, 25 ; Acts x, 22 ; Matt. i, 19.[1]

It is very striking that, according to the Synoptists,
Jesus adopted quite seriously the traditional Jewish
contrast between the righteous and the sinner : Mark
ii, 17 and par., cf. Matt. v, 45 ; Luke v, 32 ; xv, 7.
Although in fact all are called to repentance, it is
clear that the ordinary standards are recognised and
the zeal of the " righteous " is acknowledged.[2] The
same is true of Paul (Rom. v, 7, cf. ver. 6)—without
prejudice to his doctrine of justification. Jewish dis-
tinctions are not abandoned ; what the Gospels do is
to put a question mark after the word, " righteous ",
as applied to themselves by men who were hypo-
critical, complacent and scornful of others (Luke
xviii, 14 ; xvi, 15 ; cf. p. 60 (c) (d)). The retention
of the Pharisaic belief in the resurrection of the
righteous (Luke xiv, 14 ; cf. Acts xxiv, 15) shows the
persistence of this fundamental distinction, which is

---

[1] Joseph's behaviour is fundamentally that of a righteous man.
Cf. Schlatter, Matt. p. 13, differing from Billerbeck I, 50 f.,
where the reference is limited to fulfilment of the Law.

[2] Schlatter, Matt. 194, 309 ; Zahn, Matt. *ad loc.*

valid even at the Last Judgment, as it is for Paul.
The context of Luke xiv, 14 shows that love is the
ultimate test.[1]

(iv) The Christian is δίκαιος in the sense that he
fulfils the Law, doing God's will. The righteous
man (Matt. x, 41) has God's approval, and he who
receives him because he is righteous, shares in his
reward.[2] "Righteous" means "Christian" at Matt.
xiii, 43, 49,[3] as contrasted with "them that do iniquity (ἀνομίαν)", ver. 41. See also Matt. xxv, 37, 46.
The O.T. colouring of Luke i, 17 should not blind us
to the Messianic promise that the disobedient will
receive the mind of the righteous who obey God.
The righteous in James v, 6, 16 are poor Christians
suffering violence at the hands of rich enemies.[4]
Like the godly of the O.T., Christians are contrasted
with the ungodly and with sinners : I Pet. iii, 12 ;
iv, 18 ; Heb. xii, 23 ; Rev. xxii, 11. What makes
them righteous, it remains for Paul to say.

(v) Paul, as we have noted (p. 22), occasionally
retains the ordinary contrast of righteous with unrighteous, quite apart from his new doctrine of
justification, which itself starts from the self-evident
demand to do the will of God (see Rom. ii, 13), as

[1] On the question of general or partial resurrection, see Bill. IV,
1167 ff. ; Bousset-Gressmann 272 (1st ed. 256 ff.) ; E. Klostermann, Luke 151. Josephus knows only the resurrection of the
righteous, but does not represent the full Pharisaic position
(Bill. IV, 1188 f.). The Lucan tradition can hardly be said to
be inconsistent, since Luke xiv, 14 only mentions the righteous
because they gain the reward.

[2] Schlatter, Matt. 352 ; Zahn, ad loc. ; Meyer, Ursprung I,
143.

[3] [LXX and] Theod. read συνιέντες for δίκαιοι. For Jewish
parallels to this use of Dan. xii, 3, see Schlatter, Matt. 446 ;
Bill. I, 673 f. Cf. Bevan, Driver, Montgomery ad loc.

[4] Parallels from LXX and Apocr. in the comm. of Dibelius
and Hauck.

presented in the Law. In this connexion, δίκαιος
means one whom God pronounces righteous because
he has kept the Law. But now another axiom has
to be stated, viz. that "there is none righteous, no,
not one", this being the first of a series of verses
quoted at Rom. iii, 10 from Ps. xiv and Eccles. vii, 20,
expressing universal sinfulness. Not being righteous
means not fulfilling the Law because we are under
sin. To become righteous now means receiving in
faith the revealed righteousness of God as the power
of God and salvation. When Paul quotes Hab. ii, 4
at Rom. i, 17 ; Gal. iii, 11, he omits LXX μου after
πίστεως, and thus agrees substantially with the Hebrew,
" his fidelity ", but he reads a new meaning into the
old words, using " righteous " in the sense of "justified by faith ".[1] The Last Judgment is indicated at
Rom. v, 19 : "shall be placed in the class and condition of *righteous*" [Sanday and Headlam] ;[2] the
antithetical structure of this passage enables Paul here
to contrast the righteous with sinners, but he does
not go the length of saying, " we are now righteous ".
It should be noted, however, that he uses the word
at I Thess. ii, 10 to characterise the Christian life as
one of obedience to the divine law.[3]

---

[1] Lietzmann and Kühl *ad loc.* connect ἐκ πίστεως with δίκαιος
instead of with ζήσεται. But this goes against both Heb. and
LXX, and is rejected by Zahn and Preuschen-Bauer. Heb. x,
38, quoting LXX A, connects ἐκ πίστεως, in the O.T. sense
of constancy, with ζήσεται, which ver. 39 makes eschatological
(see E. Riggenbach, Heb., 2nd ed., 337 f.). For Rabbinic
treatment of Hab. ii, 4 see Schlatter, Der Glaube im N.T., 4th
ed. (1927), 609 f., Bill. III, 542 ff.

[2] E. F. K. Müller, Beobachtungen zur paulin. Rechtfertigungslehre (1905), 15. Zahn finds here a logical Future. See J de.
Zwaan, Th. St. 31 (1913), 85 ff.

[3] E. von Dobschütz, Thess. 99 ; R. C. Trench, Synonyms
(1865), 313 f.

In the wider field of Paulinism, the Christian is contrasted with the antinomians, whose weak point is their attitude to the Law,[1] as being δίκαιος (I Tim. i, 9) : no law is prescribed for him, because he judges himself according to the divine norm.[2] Among the qualifications of a bishop it is required that he should be δίκαιος (Tit. i, 8) : this means that his life must conform to the will of God, or possibly that he must be able to make right decisions.

[1] H. von Soden, Past. 2nd ed. (1893), 160 ; W. Lütgert, Die Irrlehrer der Past. (1909), 16.

[2] Cf. Rom. x, 4 ; vi, 14 f.

IV. RIGHTEOUSNESS IN THE NEW TESTAMENT

I. INTRODUCTION

In order to understand the meaning of the word δικαιοσύνη in the New Testament, it is necessary to know something of its use in the non-Christian world.

(a) Greek and Hellenistic

Δικαιοσύνη belongs to the third stage in word-formation, following δίκη and δίκαιος. Words with the termination -σύνη begin to appear in the age of abstract thought, and this explains the frequent use of the concept after the time of Homer and Hesiod, while they do not have it.[1] The linguistic development is closely connected with the growth of the Greek feeling for justice. The juridical, the ethical and the religious are vitally related to one another in the development of ideas, as the result of the domination of early Greek thought by δίκη, justice, not only in the sphere of law, but also in politics and ethics, and above all, religion (see p. 9). Four uses of δικαιοσύνη should be noted.

(i) Already in the fifth century B.C. it indicates the virtue of the citizen who behaves uprightly and does his duty. Plato adopts this : " To mind one's own business, and not be meddlesome, is justice " (Rep. iv, 433). He founds his ideal state on this, and names it with temperance as a popular and social virtue (Phaedo 82).

[1] R. Hirzel (169) thinks this due to their aristocratic tone. But that would not apply to Hesiod.

(ii) Justice is the compendium of all virtues, according to Theognis, as quoted by Aristotle (see p. 10).

(iii) Plato also mentions justice with piety, along with knowledge, courage and temperance, as a part of perfection (Prot. 330*b*) (see p. 13).

(iv) The mystical hymn in Corp. Herm. xiii, 18 calls upon Justice with Temperance to offer praise. The virtue is here transformed into a moral force, which is communicated to the re-born.   (See p. 57 and note.)

The fundamental idea among the Greeks is that δικαιοσύνη, like all other virtues, is natural to man. Cf. Aristotle, Eth. Nic. VI, xiii, 1144*b*, 27, and see p. 14.

Aristotle shows the close connexion between the idea of justice and general ethics in his definition of δικαιοσύνη as the virtue through which every man possesses that which belongs to him according to the law (Rhet. I, ix, 1366*b*, 9 ff.).   He is here harking back to the thought of the judge, who awards to each his due. Solon played an important part in the development of the idea by his insistence on distributive justice.[1]   A forensic reference thus continued to belong to the word, though it did not colour all its uses, after moral philosophy had generalised the idea.   Thus δικαιοσύνη is not only the virtue of the good citizen, but also legislative and judicial justice (Plato Gorg. 464*c* ; Aristot. Pol. IV, iv, 1291*a*, 27).   Aristotle discusses its relation to ἐπιείκεια (equity) in Eth. Nic. V, xiv, 1137*a*, 31 ff.

In a few instances δικαιοσύνη means "correctness" : Clem. Al. Strom. VI, iv, 36, 2 (cubit of *c*.) ; Deut. xxxiii, 19, Ps. iv, 5, (6), li, 19 (l, 21) (sacrifice of *c*.) ; Ps. xxiii (xxii), 3 (paths of *c*.).   These all represent the Hebrew *çedheq*.

Josephus does not use δικαιοσύνη very often, and

[1] Cf. W. Jaeger, Solons Eunomie, S.A.B. 1926, 69-85.

when he does, it is usually in the Hellenistic sense
meaning virtuous human behaviour, or even one of
the virtues, though he retains the Jewish attitude to
the Law as divine : " The reason why the con-
stitution of this legislation was ever better directed
to the utility of all than other legislations were is this,
that Moses did not make religion a part of virtue,
but he saw and he ordained other virtues to be a
part of religion—I mean justice and fortitude and
temperance and a universal agreement of the members
of the community with one another ; for all our
actions and studies, and all our words, have a reference to piety towards God " (Apion II, 170 f.,
Whiston II, xvii). The Greek point of view is clearly
implied when Josephus says that Samuel was opposed
to monarchy " because of his innate justice " (διὰ τὴν
σύμφυτον δικαιοσύνην : Ant. VI, 36, Whiston VI, iii).

Philo's only treatment of the righteousness of God
is in Deus Imm. 79, where he speaks of it as one among
other virtues in Stoic fashion. He has a striking
parallel to Rom. iii, 25 f. in Vit. Mos. II, 237 : πρὸς
ἐπίδειξιν ἀληθείας καὶ δικαιοσύνης, though the words
have not their Pauline meaning, but refer to revelation
in answer to prayer. In general, Philo's usage corresponds to the teaching of the Law, δικαιοσύνη being
the Lawgiver's main concern : Spec. Leg. IV, 143.
He takes over from the Pythagoreans the idea that
equality (ἰσότης) is the " mother " of justice : Spec.
Leg. IV, 231. Philo's exposition of δικαιοσύνη as a
virtue is more elaborate than that of Josephus ; he
calls it the queen (ἡγεμονίς) of the cardinal virtues
(see p. 13). His warmest religious interest is evident
when he is pursuing the psychological and the mystical within the limits of Platonic and Stoic tradition.
This is the case when the rise of δικαιοσύνη in the
soul is under investigation : it can be said to be there

when the three parts of the soul are in harmony, when reason guides spirit and appetite, like a man driving two horses. Clement of Alexandria (Strom. IV, xxvi, 163, 4) copies this figure—which comes originally from Plato (Phaedr. 253*d* and Rep. IV, 443*d*) and Posidonius. The effect of δικαιοσύνη in the soul is healing (Det. Pot. Ins. 123), peace (ib. 122), joy (Leg. All. III, 247), reason and asceticism playing the chief part (Det. Pot. Ins. 121 f.). In spite of the assertion that virtue is a gift from God (Sacr. A.C. 56 f.), ideas of merit still prevail (Leg. All. III, 77), and faith is the product of righteousness (Rer. Div. Mer. 93-95).[1]

(b) Septuagint

(i) The righteousness of God, as expressed by the words *çedheq* and *çᵉdhaqah*, as we have seen, has in the Old Testament an extraordinary wealth of meaning (see pp. 4-6). This certainly includes the thought of consistent, normal behaviour on the part of God—though the norm never stands over him, he is himself the norm—as is urged by Diestel and Kautzsch on etymological grounds, but this is far from exhausting the meaning of the term. The first point to be established is that *çᵉdhaqah* belongs to the terminology of relationship. He is just who does justice to claims made upon him in the name of a relationship. Thus God's righteousness is manifested first in that he rules according to the covenant in fellowship with his people.[2] This concrete, rather than abstract, way of conceiving it, means that it

[1] In one place only (Spec. Leg. IV, 181) δικαιοσύναι means righteous acts ; cf. LXX Ezek. iii, 20 ; Dan. ix, 18 ; Ecclus. xliv, 10 ; Tob. ii, 14 ; II Clem. vi, 9.

[2] Cf. W. Eichrodt, Theol. des A.T. (1933), 121 ff. It was H. Cremer, above all, who explained *çᵉdhaqah* as a term of relationship.

includes both a forensic and a soteriological element. The former was unduly minimised by Diestel and Ritschl in their reaction against the older orthodoxy, both Catholic and Protestant. But the thought of judicial righteousness, with retribution, rewards and punishments, cannot be separated from the rule of him who is both King and Judge. This is specially characteristic of Is. xl-lv, where the argument again and again is couched in the language of a lawsuit (cf. "justified" in xliii, 9, 26): Yahwe's judicial righteousness secures justice for his oppressed people in the proceedings against their conquerors; "he that justifieth" (Is. l, 8 f.) makes justice to triumph. Cf. Is. lviii, 2, where *mishpaṭ* is a synonym for *çᵉdhaqah*.

This leads directly to the thought of God's judgment and righteousness as bringing help and salvation—e.g. Deut. xxxii, 4, 35 f.; Hos. ii, 19 (21); Mic. vii, 9. Kindness, truth, loyalty, salvation are coupled with righteousness, specially in Is. xl-lv and Psalms. God's saving act, and loyalty to the Covenant, are represented as righteousness : Jer. i, 7; Is. xli, 2, 10; xlii, 6; xlv, 8; li, 5. Yahwe reveals to his people the way of salvation prescribed by his righteousness. LXX corresponds exactly to the Heb. when it explains δικαιοσύνη by σωτηρία, etc. : Ps. lxv, 5 (lxiv, 6); lxxi (lxx), 15 f.; xcviii (xcvii), 2 f.; Is. xlvi, 12 f.; li, 5; lix, 17; lxi, 10 f. The same idea is conveyed negatively in Ps. lxix, 27 (lxviii, 28); cf. Is. xlv, 23-25. The root of this coupling of justice with salvation is to be found in the idea of the covenant.

The equation of righteousness with the gift of salvation becomes even more explicit when LXX employs δικαιοσύνη as the translation of *ḥeṣedh* (Gen. xix, 19; xx, 13; xxi, 23; xxiv, 27; xxxii, 10; Exod. xv, 13; xxxiv, 7; Prov. xx, 28–LXX 22), the usual rendering being ἔλεος[1] (Ps. xxxvi, 10–LXX xxxv, 11 ; etc.). Δικαιοσύνη also stands for 'ᵉmeth, loyalty to the covenant : Gen. xxiv, 49 ; Is. xxxviii, 19 ; xxxix, 8 ; Dan. viii, 12. But the forensic reference is often found in LXX, as when it stands beside κρίσις and κρίμα, and can even, occasionally, itself represent mishpaṭ (Is. lxi, 8 ; Mal. ii, 17) ; apart from those cases in which the emphasis is soteriological, it represents the purely judicial righteousness of God : Ps. ix, 5 ; xxxv (xxxiv), 24 ; xcvi (xcv), 13.

(ii) Human righteousness consists in doing God's will. Its opposite is lawlessness (ἀνομία) : Is. v, 7. It is often coupled with truth (I Kings iii, 6), as it is when used of God (Zech. viii, 8). Cf. Test. Gad. iii, 1 and Eph. v, 9, where it means good behaviour.

(c) Synagogue

(i) The righteousness of God in the sense of Rom. iii, 21 is not known in the Synagogue.[2] A typical specimen of the Rabbinical interpretation is seen in the case of Deut. xxxiii, 21, where çidhqath Yahwe is said to be executed by Moses, as bestowing benefits like Yahwe,[3] or earning merit in the eyes of Yahwe,[4] or giving righteous judgment.[5] (LXX misunderstands the passage, and makes Yahwe the subject.) On the other hand, the Messiah is often spoken of as the righteous one, or as righteousness (see pp. 18 f.).

---

[1] Ḥeṣedh is generally rendered ἔλεος ; but this is not satisfactory, since, like çᵉdhaqah, it denotes a mutual relation of rights and duties, and particularly the obligation of loving service which springs from some form of fellowship, e.g. tribe, friendship, league. See N. Glueck, Das Wort ḥeṣedh im A.T. Sprachgebrauch, Beih. Z.A.W. 47 (1927) ; [W. F. Lofthouse, Ḥen and Ḥeṣedh in the Old Testament, Z.A.W. 1933, 31-35 ; C. H. Dodd, The Bible and the Greeks (1935), 59-65).]

[2] Billerbeck III, 163.

[3] Sifre, Deut. 355 on xxxiii, 21, Billerbeck III, 163.

[4] Targ. Onq. *ad loc.*   [5] Sifre, Deut. *loc. cit.*

Occasionally, in eschatological passages referring to the Messiah, righteousness means mercy.[1]

(ii) Righteousness as human activity. Rabbinical usage significantly narrowed down the meaning of *çᵉdhaqah* (Aram. *çidhqah*) to the giving of alms, as the most important way of fulfilling the law.[2] Private benevolence (*çᵉdhaqah* or *miçwah*) is one of the most meritorious of good works.[3] This limitation frequently appears in Rabbinical exposition of the O.T.[4] The Rabbinic parallel to ποιεῖν ἐλεημοσύνην (Matt. vi, 2) is *çidhqah 'asah* or *miçwah 'asah*.[5] LXX again and again has ἐλεημοσύνη for *çᵉdhaqah* : Deut. vi, 25 ; xxiv, 13 ; Ps. xxiv (xxiii), 5 ; xxxiii (xxxii), 5 ; ciii (cii), 6 : Is. i, 27 ; xxviii, 17 ; lix, 16 ; Dan. iv, 24 ; ix, 16 Theod. ; cf. Ecclus. iii, 30 ; vii, 10 ; xvi, 14. Almsgiving must be meant by *çᵉdhaqah* in Prov. x, 2, though LXX has δικαιοσύνη : cf. Tob. iv, 10 ; xii, 9 ; xiv, 11.

(iii) The background of the Rabbinic and LXX doctrine is the theory of merit : every act of obedience (*miçwah*) earns merit (*zakhuth*) for the Israelite in the sight of God.[6] The latter term means originally "righteousness", and the verb, *zakhah*, means to be righteous, worthy, deserving.[7] The piling up of good works becomes an end in itself.[8] Almsgiving, works of charity, the merit of the fathers—all supplement

[1] Jer. Shebi. 35c, 31 ; Midr. Ps. xxii, § 32 (99a), Billerbeck II, 575.   [2] Billerbeck I, 387 f.

[3] Ib. IV, 12, 536 ff.

[4] E.g. II Sam. viii, 15 (T. Sanh. i, 2 ff., Bill. III, 210) ; Prov. xxi, 3, 21 (Bab. Sukk. 49b, Bill. I, 500 ; Bab. Bab. B. 9b, 10b, Bill. III, 525 ; Gen. Rabb. 58 on xxiv, 19, Bill. IV, 561c) ; Is. xxxii, 17 (Ab. ii, 7, Bill. I, 387) ; Is. lix, 17 (Bab. Bab. B. 9b, Bill. III, 618) ; Hos. x, 12 (Bab. Sukk. 49b, Bill. III, 451).

[5] Bab. Gitt. 7a ; Lev. Rabb. 34 on xxv, 39, Bill. I, 388.

[6] Bill. I, 251.

[7] Ib. IV, 10. Cf. Bab. Ber. 28b ; Bab. Bab. B, 10b Bar., Bill. II, 254.   [8] Ib. IV, 6.

the keeping of the commandments.[1] A man's standing before God is settled by striking a balance between his good deeds and his transgressions.[2] If the former outweigh the latter, he is acquitted at the Last Judgment.[3] Everything depends on which way he scales turn.[4] (See p. 58 (*d*).)

(iv) The divine judgment and mercy stand immediately side by side in Ps. Sol., where God's righteousness is his just judgment (ii, 16 ; iii, 5 ; iv, 28 ; viii, 29-31 ; ix, 3, 7 ; cf. ii, 12, 19, 36 ; iii, 3 ; v, 1 ; viii, 27 ; x, 6 ; xvii, 3).[5] Along with this appears kindness, mercy, grace, without any indication of the relation between the two (ii, 40 ; v, 2, 17 ; vii, 4 f., 8, 9 ; viii, 33 f. ; ix, 15 f. ; x, 8 ; xi, 2, 9). The thought of salvation is expressed by ἔλεος and χάρις, but not by δικαιοσύνη (see p. 58 (*f*)).

Jubilees similarly combines God's kindness and mercy (x, 3) with his righteousness, which is predominantly judicial (xxi, 4).[6] But Jub. differs from Ps. Sol. in that it can speak of "salvation in righteousness" (i, 15), and joins mercy and judgment more closely together (xxxi, 25).[7] But here also no attempt is made to explain the connexion between the two ideas.

II Esdras viii, 36, on the other hand, comes very near to the language of Paul : "In this, O Lord, thy righteousness and thy goodness shall be declared, if thou be merciful unto them which have no store of good works". Such a statement is unthinkable in Ps. Sol., and represents a very late type of Judaism.

[1] Bill. IV, 6. [2] Ib. I, 251. [3] Ib. IV, 5.
[4] Jer. Qidd., 61*d*, 47, Bill. IV, 11.
[5] God's chastening (παιδεύειν) of Israel is frequently coupled with his mercy : vii, 3-5 ; viii, 32-35, etc. The righteousness in which the Messiah is to rule (xvii, 28) is his spotlessness in the sight of God.
[6] At Jub. xxv, 1, and xxx, 20, δικαιοσύνη means good human behaviour. [7] So also En. xxxix, 5 ; lxxi, 3.

The Rabbinical word for legal right is not *çᵉdhaqah*
but *din*. There was much discussion in the Synagogue about the relationship between God's judgment
and his mercy. The two were sharply contrasted as
middath haddin and *middath haraḥᵃmin*.[1] It is frequently
stated that kindness exceeds severity.[2] When pardon
is granted, mercy restrains wrath and displaces punitive
justice.[3] Thus in Gen. xviii, 19, *çᵉdhaqah* is interpreted as mercy, and *mishpaṭ* as justice (cf. *din* above).[4]
The problem is also reflected in the contrast between
shurath haddin and *liphnim mishshurath haddin* (judicial
strictness and indulgence).[5] Kindliness ranks higher
among men than mere legality,[6] and God himself is
said to be indulgent.[7] But it always remains un-
certain among the Rabbis, a matter of *pro* and *con*,
whether God will be just or merciful.

2. NEW TESTAMENT : NON-PAULINE

(*a*) Δικαιοσύνη as just judgment and government.
A few passages use the word for God's righteous
judgment through the returning Christ : Acts xvii,
31 ; Rev. xix, 11 ; cf. the revelation of retributive
justice through Christ in the Freer logion at Mark
xvi, 14 ; it means God's just government of the

[1] Mek. on Exod. xv, 2, Bill. I, 1042 ; Gen. Rab. 12 on ii, 4
(end), Bill. III, 292 ; Midr. Shir i, 14, Bill. II, 279 ; Gen.
Rab. 65 on xxvii, 1, Bill. III, 694.

[2] Bab. Sanh. 100a Bar., Bill. I, 444 ; Sifra Lev. on v, 17,
Bill. III, 230 ; T. Sotah iv, 1. On the appeal to severity see
Gen. Rab. 45 on xvi, 5, Bill. III, 301.

[3] Bab. Ber. 7a Bar., Bill. II, 79.

[4] E.g., Gen. Rab. 49 on xviii, 19, Bill. III, 196.

[5] Bill. I, 341 ; IV, 18.

[6] Bab. Bab. Q. 99b, Bill. iv, 19, cf. 15 ; Mek. on Exod.
xviii, 20, Bill. I, 345.

[7] Bab. Ber. 7a Bar., Bill. II, 79 ; Deut. Rab. 4 on x, 1, Bill.
IV, 18.

Christian community [giving equal privileges to all]
at II Pet. i, 1 ; and the justice of judges and kings
at Heb. xi, 33.   " The word of righteousness " (Heb.
v, 13) means " regular, normal speech ".[1]

(b) Δικαιοσύνη as doing right in the sight of God.
Apart from the passages just mentioned, and the
Pauline usage, with its special formula, " the righteousness of God ", it may be stated generally that in
the New Testament righteousness means almost
always human behaviour in harmony with God's
will, and well-pleasing to him—uprightness of life,
doing what is right in God's sight.   This is differ-
entiated from Greek and Hellenistic moral ideas, and
closely related to the Old Testament, by its constant
reference to God and its vital connexion with his
mighty acts.

(i) Matthew always uses the word in this sense.
The baptism of Jesus (iii, 15) is to fulfil all duty to
God,[2] not " every ordinance " (δικαίωμα).[3]   There is
no need to take the fourth beatitude (v, 6) as referring
to the judging and saving righteousness of God, in
a forensic, eschatological sense.[4]   On the other hand,
it is quite clear that righteousness is here not a matter
of merit, as with the Jews, but a free gift of God to
those who earnestly desire it.[5]   " His Kingdom and
righteousness " (vi, 33) means that which will bring
the disciples into perfect harmony with God's will.
Again it is a gift, like everything connected with the
Kingdom.

[1] Riggenbach, Hab. 144 f.   Cf. δικαιοσύνη as substantive of
δίκαιος, " correct " (see pp. 15 and 27).

[2] Schlatter, Matt. 89 ff.   Cf. on Matt. iii, 15, A. Friedrichsen
in Revue d'histoire et de Philos. Relig. VII (1927), 245 ff.

[3] Zahn, Matt. 140, cf. Zahn, Einleitung, 3rd ed., II, 318, n. 10.
So also Klostermann ad. loc., Preuschen-Bauer, 306.

[4] Cremer, Paul. Rechtfertigungslehre 190.

[5] Schlatter, Matt. 136 f. ; Bill. I, 201 f.

4

The parallelism with Paul's gospel of justification is here as obvious as it is in all the other passages in which Matthew emphasises the merciful saving of sinners.[1] Doing right before God leads to persecution (v, 10). It must exceed the righteousness of the Pharisees.[2] Matt. vi, 1 uses "righteousness" as a general heading for a number of pious observances.[3] These do not exhaust the meaning of the term, but they provide characteristic examples of righteousness as that which is done in the sight of God and for his sake. John the Baptist came in the way of righteousness (xxi, 32), and therefore called for conduct in harmony with God's will. (For "way", cf. Job xxiv, 13 ; Prov. viii, 20 ; xii, 28 ; xvi, 31 ; xvii, 23 ; xxi, 16, 21.)

(ii) Luke agrees with Matthew. The Benedictus, in the emotional language of liturgy, speaks of serving God in holiness and righteousness before him (i, 75). The association of the two words is suggestive of Greece (cf. Wis. ix, 3 ; Josh. xxiv, 14, LXX), but "righteousness before him" is something bigger than a Greek virtue. The distinction between "moral" and "religious" does not hold. This means the fulfilment of God's will by doing what pleases him. Acts brings out the point that God seeks this in the Gentile world (xiii, 10 ; xxiv, 25), and recognises it wherever it is found (x, 35)—though it should be

---

[1] Cf. R. Bultmann, Die Bedeutung des geschichtl. Jesus für die Theologie des Paulus, Th. Bl. VIII (1929), 143.

[2] Schlatter takes Matt. v, 20 to mean going further beyond the letter of the Law than the Pharisees (Matt. 159 ff.). It is simpler to regard ἐὰν μὴ περισσεύσῃ πλεῖον as an emphatic comparative. Cf. Dalman, Jesus-Jeshua (1922, Eng. trans. 1929), 67 ff.

[3] The reading δικαιοσύνην (Sin B D Syr Sin) is preferable to ἐλεημοσύνην.

noted that something more is needed for salvation, viz. forgiveness of sins (x, 43).

(iii) Similarly, in I and II Peter, righteousness is always doing right so as to please God. It is made possible by deliverance from sin through the Cross (I Pet. ii, 24)—as Paul also says (Rom. vi ; see p. 53). As in Matt. v, 10, it will involve suffering (iii, 14). Noah, as a herald of righteousness (II Pet. ii, 5), represents the life of obedience to God over against the world of the ungodly. The way of righteousness is shown by the holy commandment (ii, 21). The new world will be the home of righteousness (iii, 13 ; cf. p. 19).

(iv) Hebrews also presents the same picture, apart from the two Hellenistic phrases noted above (p. 35). The quotation from Ps. xlv (xliv), 8 is used (Heb. i, 9) to show Christ's exaltation as the reward for his life of righteousness. Melchizedek means "king to whom righteousness belongs " (vii, 2) ; it is as such that he is a type of Christ. The righteousness of which Noah became heir (xi, 7) has not a forensic meaning, but refers to the godly life which corresponds to faith.[1] Hebrews here—like Matthew—agrees with Paul that righteousness is a gift. As a fruit of chastening (xii, 11), righteousness means a life fully conformed to God's will.

(v) The only difference between John and the foregoing is that he shows, more clearly than Matt. iii, 15 and Hebrews, the vital bearing of Christ's righteous life on the whole conception of righteousness. He does this by means of his Christology, so that righteousness is inseparable from the Christ as the righteous one. Jesus is set forth as having this character in his resurrection and exaltation (John xvi, 8, 10).

[1] $K\alpha\tau\acute{\alpha}$ is a periphrasis for the Genitive. Cf. Riggenbach, 352 f.

Accordingly, the doing of righteousness is the practice and confirmation of that which is embodied in him, and therefore evidence of being begotten of God (I John ii, 29).[1] Those who are antinomian on the ground that he is righteous are exhorted to imitate him, avoiding sin (iii. 7 f.) ; and this means brotherly love (iii, 10). See also Rev. xxii, 11.

Do the passages so far adduced show the way to righteousness in the sight of God ? Matthew says clearly that it is a gift of the Kingdom of God, and I Peter (ii, 24) connects it impressively with deliverance from sin through the Cross. This points definitely, though not dogmatically, in the direction of Pauline doctrine. John also connects true righteousness exclusively with the revelation in Christ, by making it the result of union with him as the righteous one. But Israel's old problem of justification before God was only really settled by James and Paul.

(c) Δικαιοσύνη in James. The "righteousness of God" of James i, 20, cannot be identified with Paul's watchword, which conveys the essence of his doctrine of salvation through the Cross. The reference must be to works of righteousness, which is said to be of God because its definition and demand are from him alone. Such works cannot be wrought by human wrath, which is irreconcilably opposed to the righteousness of God. What is remarkable is that this saying puts good works under the heading of divine, and not of human, righteousness. This is well on the way towards Paul's concern for subjection to the righteousness of God (Rom. x, 3).[2] "The fruit of righteousness" (iii, 18 ; cf. Prov. iii, 9 ; xi, 30, etc.; Am. vi, 12) means the righteousness which is the

[1] Cf. II Sam. viii, 15 ; Ps. cvi (cv), 3 ; Is. lvi, 1 ; lviii, 2 ; Ps. Sol. ix, 5.

[2] Cf. Schlatter, Jak. 51, 142.

harvest of a life devoted to the will of God. (Genitive of apposition or content.)

While James thus shares the prevailing view of those parts of the N.T. so far considered, he goes beyond them when he says of Abraham, " it was reckoned unto him for righteousness " (ii, 23),[1] providing an answer to the question concerning the way to righteousness before God—the way of salvation. This hotly disputed passage brings us close to Paul's great subject of justification. (For the word ἐλογίσθη, " was reckoned ", see Gen. xv, 6 ; Ps. cvi (cv), 31 ; I Macc. ii, 52 ; Jub. xiv, 6 ; xxxi, 23 ; xxx, 17 ; xxxv, 2 ; Philo Rer. Div. Her. xc, 94 ; Abr. 262.)

The subject is treated polemically, and an attack made upon the dead orthodoxy, which certainly talks about " faith ", but is not interested in work. A strong point is therefore made of the marriage of faith with work. The reference is not to carrying out the details of the Law in a Rabbinical sense, but to practical love and obedience, the sort of thing that Paul describes as the fruit of the Spirit, the hall-mark of a Christian. The whole epistle teaches the same lesson, which is as far removed from the Jewish idea of earning merit as from Greek ethics. James simply demands, in a direct, untheological way, that faith shall not be distorted into a substitute for work. Abraham is righteous in God's sight because he is credited with the faith that is accompanied and perfected by work (ii, 23). It is perfectly true that this way of putting it is more like the Jewish view than Paul's way, lacking, as it does, the contrast between grace and works ; and it cannot be denied that James here presents a conception of faith which

[1] Cf. comm. of Dibelius 168, Windisch 20 f., Hauck 124 ff., Schlatter 51-60, 202 f. ; A. Meyer, Rätsel des Jak. (1930), 86 ff. ; [J. Moffatt in D.A.C. II, 373*b*].

differs "theologically" from that of Paul. But it must be remembered that this is a popular piece of practical polemics, directed against the attempt to set up a doctrine of faith without work, and has nothing to do with what Paul says about faith "apart from the works of the Law". The remark about demons believing (ii, 19) is not the only thing James has to say about faith. An examination of the whole collection of his sayings in this epistle shows that fundamentally faith means more to him than that bit of orthodoxy. At the same time it must be granted that Paul could never have stood for the contention that Abraham was justified on the ground of the work which accompanied and authenticated his faith. James is not here concerned with the judgment through which all works must pass, whether enjoined by the Law or not; nor does he touch on the aspects of the subject presented at Matt. vi, 33 and I Pet. ii, 24 (see pp. 35 and 38). But his exhortation, in spite of the disputable theology of ii, 23, is at one with the general doctrine of the early Church in its plea for a faith which produces the right kind of behaviour.[1]

3. PAUL

(a) Origin and basis of the Pauline gospel of justification. In order to understand what Paul means by "the righteousness of God", we must go back to the Law, which he calls a law of righteousness because it demands righteousness (Rom. ix, 30). "Moses writeth that the man that doeth the righteous-

---

[1] Schlatter (Jak. 51 ff.) suggests that "apart from works" is a development from the earlier Pauline "apart from works of the Law", comparable with Corinthian libertinism. This is illuminating, but does not relieve the tension due to the fact that James includes works in the reckoning.

ness which is of the Law shall live thereby " (Rom.
x, 5 ; cf. Test. Dan vi, 10, where the first Slavonic
version adds "of the Law"; Apoc. Bar. li, 3 ;
lxiii, 3 ; lxvii, 6) : i.e. it is a condition of life.   But
that stage in the plan of salvation is past ; there is
now actually no " righteousness which is of the Law ".
It is true that a relative perfection may be attained
(Phil. iii, 6), but Paul has come to understand that
the Law cannot produce true righteousness before
God (Gal. iii, 21).   The self-righteousness which it
does produce (Rom. x, 3 ; Phil. iii, 9) is only " loss "
and " refuse " (Phil. iii, 8).   See further Gal. ii, 21 ;
Titus iii, 5.[1]

Paul reaches the new truth of the " righteousness
of God " in the effort to define his position in relation
to the Law.   But it cannot be said [2] that his gospel
of justification [3] owes more to that effort than to his
personal spiritual experience.   No doubt this is the
crucial point in his discussion with Judaism.   He
speaks in a different way to the Corinthians.   But he
is under the necessity of clarifying his position to
himself, and the question of the Law is fundamental
for his whole theology.   What is commonly called the
" mysticism " of Paul cannot be separated from the
new relationship to God, brought about apart from
the Law.   Justification became the battle-cry of his
mission because it expressed a new understanding of
the relation of Christ to the Law.   Paul uses the
sacred word of Judaism—righteousness—in the service
of his polemic against the Jewish conception of the
Law.

[1] On works of the Law cf. E. Lohmeyer, Probl. paulin. Theol.
II, Z.N.W., 28 (1929), 177 ff.

[2] As by A. Meyer, op. cit. 99 f., following Wrede, Paulus
(1904), 72 ff.

[3] Cf. H. E. Weber, " Eschatologie " und " Mystik " im N.T.,
100 f.

The presupposition of Paul's message is the O.T. idea of God, as the Judge, who demands obedience and distributes rewards and punishments. It is also fundamental with him that man is the slave of sin, and guilty before God. But he goes right away from Judaism in his radical rejection of the optimism which believes it possible to fulfil the Law. This is bound up with the complete collapse of Rabbinical piety in his own life. He still believes that only the righteous can have true fellowship with God ; but according to the Gospel no effort on man's part can qualify him for this fellowship ; God's sovereign grace alone can do that, taking action in Christ on behalf of mankind.

(b) The full formula, " righteousness of God ", is used by Paul in his most solemn and striking utterances on the subject of salvation ; elsewhere he speaks simply of righteousness. In the former, there can be no doubt that θεοῦ is to be understood as a subjective Genitive. God's righteousness is exclusively his own, and man is brought into it and given a place within it.[1] The righteousness of God is judgment and mercy in one ; it belongs to him, and he

---

[1] So rightly O. Zanker 399, 418. In the discussion of " the righteousness of God " A. Ritschl and L. Diestel lay proper emphasis on salvation, but neglect the forensic element, which is recognised by A. Schmitt 129. Zahn identifies it with Christ ; but the exceptional statement of I Cor. i, 30 should not be generalised. Kühl takes it, too formally, to mean the objective norm set forth in the Gospel. Lietzmann leaves the question open : either God's own righteousness or that which he imputes. [But see his " The Beginnings of the Christian Church ", 2nd ed. (trans. B. L. Woolf, 1949), 115 f. : " God is righteous and makes righteous ".] The most important contributions to the discussion are those of Kölbing and Haering, who apprehend the twofold nature of the idea, combining the redemptive and the judicial, though they limit the former to the atoning death, under the influence of Ritschl.

manifests it in what he does when he imparts it in absolving the sinner ; but it also inaugurates a new life of duty in the service of the King ; its perfect demonstration is at the Last Judgment. (Cf. Deut. xxxiii, 21 ; Od. Sol. xxv. 10 ; II Esdr. viii, 36.)

The main features of the gospel of justification are as follows.

(i) The whole of mankind forms the setting of the righteousness of God ; it is not simply a matter of individual experience, but primarily an act of God in Christ, affecting the human race as a whole (Rom. i-iii).

(ii) God's righteousness is more than an attribute, in the static sense of Hellenistic ethics, or as in the older Protestant theology. It is dynamic—as active as his wrath (Rom. i, 17 f. ; iii, 5, 21, 25 f.).

(iii) The saving act of propitiation (ἱλαστήριον, see p. 61 n.) was performed at a particular place (Rom. iii, 25 f. ; v, 9 f. ; cf. II Cor. v, 18 ; Gal. iii, 13), at a particular time (Rom. iii, 21, 26), viz. at the Cross of Christ, which marks the end of the way of the Law (iii, 21). But the Resurrection always goes along with the Cross ; for this is more than a formal declaration in the unseen world. The Cross as the mighty act of God in history forms the keystone of Paul's closely-knit argument. Hence it is possible to use the formula, found only at 1 Cor. i, 30 (see p. 42, n. 1)—" Christ was made righteousness and sanctification and redemption ". There is no need to give δικαιοσύνη, which is unmistakably regarded here as the foundation, a meaning different from that which it has in Galatians and Romans.[1] A similar personification, so to speak, is involved in Rom. x, 4.

(iv) God both is and imparts righteousness. Paul's formula means that God is just, righteousness belongs

[1] With Schmiedel, I Cor. 77, but not J. Weiss, I Cor. 41.

to him ; not, however, in the sense of a mere attribute, but as something actually put forth in the showing of his judgment (Rom. iii, 25 f.). This is certainly a manifestation of God's mercy, but at the same time it is an uncompromising putting forth of his righteousness as judge. It is attested in an act of atonement, and makes it impossible to misunderstand the " passing over of the sins done aforetime ".[1] Cf. the linking of the idea of judgment with what God did at the Cross in Gal. iii, 13 ; II Cor. v, 21 ; Rom. viii, 3. At the same time, ἔνδειξις is the granting of the absolution that saves the sinner.[2] It says two things, has two sides—is, in fact, the marrying of judgment and mercy. Judaism had wrestled in vain with the problem of adjusting these to each other (see p. 34), with only an occasional glimpse of the hope that God's sympathy might get the better of his severity. When Paul sees God's act in the Cross, he is convinced, with the absolute certainty of faith, that this is the final and effectual revelation of justice and mercy in one. This rules out unconditionally the antinomian misunderstanding of moral laxity and feeble compromise. Forgiveness as a genuine act of judgment, maintaining God's justice, is a form of redemption which knows no compromise with evil. The legalistic Pharisee speaks of the Law as disclosing the demand of God's righteousness ; Paul the Pharisee, apprehended by Christ, goes on to speak of the Cross as making known its work of judgment and mercy.

(v) Justification in the forensic sense is included in " the righteousness of God ". The believer is pronounced righteous and is given a new character in the sight of God. The divine judgment produces

---

[1] This cannot refer to pre-baptismal sins (Mundle, Der Glaubensbegriff des Paulus 88) ; its context is the history of salvation.　　　[2] N.B. Rom. iii, 19 : " under judgment ".

righteousness in the believer through absolution (see pp. 61 and 70, and note the contrast with condemnation in Rom. viii, 34 and II Cor. iii, 9, cf. xi, 15). " Forensic " does not mean that the sinner is treated as if he were righteous, for God's sovereign judicial declaration produces an actual effect. Nor does it mean the setting up of a moral ideal to be striven after. What is indicated is that he who has righteousness is right with God. Law court language is really only used parabolically for being what one ought to be before God, and legal corollaries ought not to be pressed. This is not a case of human judicial proceedings, for the divine Judge is at the same time the omnipotent King. We certainly have to do with a picture, just as when words like " reconciliation " are used, but its glorious meaning is not to be apprehended by working out the logical implications of the legal metaphor. We must pass at once from the law court into the presence of God. The *justificatio injusti* is contrary to all the rules of human justice. The illustration is inadequate for the reality. This act of mercy goes far beyond all ordinary legal procedure. As a judicial pronouncement, it is incomparable of its kind. But what chiefly claims our attention is the underlying motif : the sole purpose of the use of legal terminology is to make it clear that the grace of God is not something arbitrary and capricious, but that it operates according to the principles of the holy Covenant, and is in perfect harmony with his justice. Objection could only be taken to the legal metaphor if it implied the Pharisaic doctrine of merit in such a way as to prejudice the holiness of God. The picture of the judge is admissible, because, in spite of its shortcomings, the Law does express abiding divine principles ; it can be applied to God just as well as the picture of father or king, in spite of human

associations. The danger is minimised by the fact
that logically the Pauline gospel of justification is a
complete paradox.

(vi) Paul means much more than forgiveness and
reconciliation, though he occasionally uses these
expressions (Rom. iv, 7 ; v, 9 f. ; II Cor. v, 18-20).
Whereas Judaism looked for a favourable verdict at
the Last Judgment, on the ground of good works,
Paul believed in the present possession of righteousness
as a free gift of God (Rom. iii, 24-26 ; v, 1, 9, 17 ;
viii, 30 ; ix, 30 ; I Cor. vi, 11 ; cf. viii, 10 ; x, 6),
meaning not only the forgiveness of sins, but also the
effectual working of the grace of God, a radical
salvation (cf. $\varsigma^e dhaqah$ in Ps. and Is.). This is something new, and makes it possible to speak of " a state
of justification " [Westminster Confession]. Phil. iii, 9
refers to the continual renewal of this experience of
receiving righteousness through faith, emphasising the
point that it comes from God, and not from the Law
(cf. Is. liv, 17 ; Bar. v, 2, 9) : but it must not be
taken as the key to all that Paul meant by the righteousness of God ; [1] for that we must turn to Rom. i, 17 ;
iii, 21 ff. The essential point is that δικαιοσύνη θεοῦ
means both the righteousness which God has, mani-
festing it in the act of salvation, and that which, as
Saviour, he continually communicates ; however the
wording may vary, the fact remains that it is always
ultimately his righteousness alone. The state of
justification is in no sense a human achievement ; it
is the free gift of God, who draws man into his own
righteousness.

(vii) Faith is the means whereby the individual is
drawn into participation in the consequences of the
saving event. Although Paul does not exactly try to
localise personal justification, since he is not particu-

[1] So rightly Haering, p. 6.

larly interested in isolated experiences, he nevertheless
has in mind always God's action in justifying the
individual, and not only the community.[1] Actually,
he does not think of the individual as existing by himself ; when a man is justified, he becomes forthwith a
member of the Body of Christ, as formerly he belonged
to Israel, or the Gentiles, or the human race. The
gift of justification does not diminish personal obligation ; it defines it. But, over against all exaggeration
of the importance of the personal experience of justification, it is essential to insist that what is said in this
connexion is all orientated to the completely objective
fact of what God has done. This is shown in the
belief that Paul's converts were justified when they
were baptised and received the Spirit (I Cor. vi, 11 ;
Gal. iii, 6, cf. iii, 1-5).[2] But the sacrament must not
be regarded as working by magic. That is excluded
by I Cor. i, 17, and indeed by the whole Pauline conception of faith. Abraham's circumcision is similarly
" a seal of the righteousness of faith which he had
while he was in uncircumcision ". He also received
the gift of righteousness before the sacrament. Sacramental magic is ruled out (see p. 63, n. 3).

The relation of the subjective attitude to the objective act of redemption needs special explanation.
Rom. x, 3 shows that the historical manifestation of
pardoning righteousness is the very power of God,
who rules over all, and it is man's business to submit
to it. We cannot dismiss this, on the strength of Phil.
iii, 9, as meaning merely the righteousness which is
granted to the believer. This means being directly
challenged and arrested by God, brought under his

[1] Ritschl, Rechtf. u. Versöhn. III (1888), 545 f.

[2] Mundle (84 ff., 135 ff.) goes far beyond Paul when he identifies justification with transplanting into the sacramental process
of salvation.

authority, made partaker at once in the mighty act
of salvation through faith, and set within the sphere
of God's righteousness (cf. Rom. iii, 22).[1] All who
believe share in that righteousness. The demand for
faith always accompanies the most objective utterances concerning the righteousness of God (Rom.
i, 17 ; iii, 22-28 ; iv, 5, 1). The achievement and
proclamation of salvation are never separated from
the appropriation of it, and the revelation under discussion can never be taken out of the sphere of the
I–and–Thou relation. From the very beginning,
faith is an indispensable condition of the new experience. See Rom. iii, 21 ; 25 f. (διὰ πίστεως goes with
δικαιοσύνη θεοῦ) ; Phil. iii, 9.

Thus the divine objectivity in the work of salvation
is throughout relative to those who are being saved.
But the same may be said, from the opposite point
of view, concerning faith. Whereas to Philo faith is
a separable and definable property (σχέσις) of the
soul, it means for Paul man's total surrender to God's
saving act. The faith which is reckoned for righteousness is not a psychic force, or an achievement of
almighty reason, or the perfection of religious virtue
(Philo) ; it is the realisation of God alone as saviour,
the one and only way of opening the door to the
revelation of the one and only true object of faith.
The fact that different prepositions are used to link
the words δικαιοσύνη and πίστις shows that faith is
not a special kind of meritorious work (with the simple
genitives of Rom. iv, 11, 13, cf. the prepositions in
ix, 30 ; x, 6 ;[2] Phil. iii, 9) ; it is significant that
δικαιοσύνη διὰ τὴν πίστιν never occurs.[3] This con-

---

[1] The Alex. text is to be preferred [with R.V.], omitting " and
upon all ". So Lietzmann (46), but not Zahn (176).

[2] Cf. Bultmann, Der Stil der paulin. Predigt (1910), 87 f.

[3] Cf. W. Michaelis, Rechtf. aus Glauben bei Paulus (1927), 136.

clusion is confirmed by the use of the term λογίζεσθαι
(see p. 39). It is true that it indicates reckoning,
and by itself might well lead to misunderstanding,
as if righteousness could be earned (Gal. iii, 9 ; Rom.
iv, 3, 5 f., 9, 11, 22) ; but it is just by means of this
sharp antithesis that the doctrine of merit is over-
thrown. Faith comes of God ; no merit attaches to
it ; to say that it was reckoned is to exhibit the sheer
grace of the divine generosity. That which is reckoned is the creation of sovereign grace. God himself
acknowledges that in the faith he has found the full
satisfaction of justice.

(viii) Hope is an outstanding characteristic of
righteousness. The experience of salvation in the
present is a pledge of salvation in the future, for
justification is grace bridging the gap and inaugurat-
ing the world to come ; Paul's " But now " (Rom.
iii, 21) has the force of fulfilment ; what remains of
earthly life is an *interim*. Therein lies the great
revolution. Judaism put justification at the end of
the world, and was not sure of it ; the Christian
actually has it now. History offers it, and faith takes
hold of it. Imputed righteousness foreshortens time
and points to fulfilment, thus producing hope that
is beyond comparison with the vague uncertainty of
the Jew. The believer, who has found immediate
absolution at the Cross, looks forward to the Last
Judgment with confidence. This is not quietism ; it
is the dynamic of a new way of life. " The righteousness we hope for " (Gal. v, 5 [Moffatt]) is acquittal
at the Last Judgment (cf. Gal. ii, 16 ; Rom. ii, 13 ; [1]
iii, 20, 30 ; v, 19 ; viii, 33—referring to the Last
Judgment ; x, 4-10—eschatological, cf. v, 17).[2]

[1] But see p. 64.
[2] Cf. Mark xvi, Freer Logion, 22-24 : " the glory to be in-
herited, which consists of righteousness ".

Present and future are united in the association of righteousness with salvation (Rom. x, 10, etc.), the latter, like " life " (v, 17, cf. x, 10), being an eschatological term.[1] It is not that the Last Judgment is anticipated by faith,[2] but rather that it is both present and future at the same time, like redemption and adoption, as Paul understands them. The future form of expression indicates that what is given is not a static condition, but a movement towards a goal ; like all Christ's gifts, it involves the tension of hope.

Paul saw no contradiction between justification by the mercy of God and the Last Judgment according to works, which he constantly took for granted in his preaching. This was not a mere relic of Judaism,[3] like a fossil, but an organic and radical part of his doctrine,[4] enabling him to show how the present and the future are one to the believer in justification. His treatment of the subject sets the divine standard over all, and is a radical summons to the fear of God. We have already seen that the idea of God as judge is the indispensable premise to the gospel of justification. It is quite true that Paul does not devote a theological discussion to the relation between justification and the Last Judgment. But it is the judgment motif which gives its seriousness both to the new confidence and to the tireless pursuit of the goal, and guards against a false sense of security. The assurance of salvation is not thereby shaken. The thought of judgment acts as a powerful stimulant to obedience. The new faith demands repeated encounters with the relentless severity of God, as seen at the Cross. It is only the absolute standard, associated with the idea of the

[1] Cf. Haering, p. 61.
[2] Cf. Kölbing, p. 8 ff. ; Haering, pp. 58 f.
[3] The antinomy has often been thus explained, cf. Braun, 24 f.
[4] Cf. Braun, 48, 76, 94.

Last Judgment, that can preserve the understanding of the Cross from degenerating into the antinomian view that justification does away with the duty of doing the will of God. Paul does not work this out logically ; his task is to get people to press on. He has broken away completely from the pretentious eschatological calculations of Judaism. As for Luther's [1] view that when God justifies a man, he starts a process of complete renewal, assuring him of eventual perfection—this certainly is to be found in Rom. viii, 30, but not as a piece of logic or mathematics, for when God saves a man, he performs an act of creation, and that is a miracle.

(ix) Justification is closely related to Paul's so-called "mysticism". He connects it with the Spirit (I Cor. vi, 11 ; Rom. x, 8 f.), and says that both are received apart from works (Rom. iii, 28 ; Gal. iii, 2, 5). Saving faith and union with Christ in his death go together (Gal. ii, 16-21 ; iii, 26-29). The close connexion between the two appears in the unusual wording of II Cor. v, 21, where identification is substituted for imputation (cf. Jer. xxiii, 6 ; xxxiii, 16– LXX xl, 16) ; righteousness still belongs to God, but identification is very strongly expressed.[2] The juridical is combined with the mystical in Phil. iii, 7-11. In Romans generally it is impossible to separate the state of justification from being "in Christ". If we were to interpret the latter as meaning mystical union in the technical sense, we should have to accuse Paul of living a double life theologically, because justification and faith necessarily involve the idea of separation between God and man ; in fact they may

---

[1] W. A. II, 108, 3 ff. ; cf. Holl, Ges. Auf. zur Kirchengesch. I, Luther, 2nd and 3rd eds. (1923), 123 ff. ; H. J. Holtzmann, Lehrb. der N.T. Theol. 2nd ed. II (1911), 226 ff. ; Braun, 31.

[2] Windisch, II Cor. 199, sees here mystical perfectionism.

be said to be intended to guard against just such a misunderstanding. What happens is that the gift of righteousness transfers a man into fellowship with Christ. Paul's mystical terminology is used by way of illustration, and must not be pressed to its logical conclusions, any more than the illustrations from the law-court. The justification formula is one among others. The linking of the juridical with the mystical shows that the work of justification is brought to completion by the Spirit.[1]

(x) Righteousness is the power of the new life. Justification does not mean quietism at any stage ; it is always teleological, and leads to the royal rule of grace (Rom. v, 12-21), which is the sure way to eternal life. This is a rule of righteousness (ver. 21), which is not only the starting-point, but also the secret of progress, for it brings the believer within the movement of the rule of God. Statements about justification should not be separated from the life-giving Lordship of Christ (ver. 21) or from the gift of life to the community. Righteousness and life are intertwined (vv. 17, 21), and lead to life eternal, whereas sin leads to death. " Righteousness " in Rom. viii, 10 does not mean the good life, but the state of justification : the Spirit is the power of the new life.

It is a complete mistake to ascribe to Paul the idea of salvation as a process that is ended.[2] When a man is declared righteous, he enters the service of

[1] See W. Grundmann, in Z.N.W., 32 (1933), 52 ff., for argument against the view of Pfleiderer, Wrede and Schweitzer [The Mysticism of Paul the Apostle, tr. by W. Montgomery, 1931, 205-226] that the doctrine of justification is a subsidiary crater within the main doctrine of redemption through mystical union with Christ.

[2] Windisch in R.G.G., 2nd ed., II, 1204.

righteousness, becoming, so to speak, its property ; his faith in God's righteousness is obedience, and leads to obedience ; and thus there is a close parallelism between his experience and the inseparable Cross and resurrection which form the starting-point of justification. See Rom. vi, 12-23. There is no difficulty or contradiction in passing from the forensic idea of righteousness to thinking of it as the power of life which conquers sin. The gift of righteousness brings the believer into the custody of this power. Again, it is righteousness which gives admission to the state of sanctification. It takes command of the whole of life as the victor over unrighteousness and sin. Thus Paul uses δικαιοσύνη to mean both the righteousness which acquits the sinner and the life-force which breaks the bondage of sin. It is impossible to charge him with lack of interest in the good life, as if δικαιοσύνη referred only to the beginning of the Christian life, and so what we are here discussing ought to come under the heading of missionary theory. Of course Paul does not think of righteousness as actually belonging to the believer ; it is an objective norm which exercises divine authority over him ; and at the same time the word can be applied to right action (Rom. vi, 16), just as to the state of justification (see p. 46). " The armour of righteousness " (II Cor. vi, 7 : subjective Genitive) is that which is provided by the divine righteousness.[1] The Christian life bears the stamp of righteousness as opposed to iniquity (II Cor. vi, 14 [in ver. 15 Christ is the personification of righteousness]), and its ethical aspect, in the sense of Rom. vi, is emphasised at Rom. xiv, 17. " Almsgiving " might be suggested as the meaning of δικαιοσύνη in the quotations from Ps. cxii (cxi), 9,

[1] There is no analogy in Paul for Bachmann's interpretation : weapons for righteous use.

and Hos. x, 12 at II Cor. ix, 9 f., because the
context deals with the collection : but since ver. 8
speaks of " every good work ", it is more likely to
mean the goodness which expresses itself in charity.
" The fruit of righteousness " (Phil. i, 11)—whether
the Genitive is of apposition, origin or quality—is to
be understood in the sense of Rom. vi. That righteousness, as " fruit ", is the gift of God, and not just
natural goodness, is also indicated at Eph. v, 9. The
same idea is implied in " the breastplate of righteousness " (Eph. vi, 14, cf. Is. lix, 17), which means the
power regulating the life of the Christian, without
special reference to justification by faith. " Godly
behaviour " is the meaning at II Tim. iii, 16 (cf.
Bar. iv, 13), and " the crown of a good life " (II Tim.
iv, 8 [Moffatt]) is more likely to be what Paul meant
than complete acquittal at the Last Judgment. A
general review of Paul's usage shows that the formula,
" the righteousness of God ", carries with it the
conviction that at the very moment of justification
the believer is admitted into the status of righteousness in the new life : justification is the means whereby
he is brought under the creative power of the
righteousness of God.

(xi) Hellenistic moral philosophy plays no part in
the Pauline or deutero-Pauline doctrine of righteousness. The word ἀρετή (virtue) is never used in this
connexion [N.T. only has it at Phil. iv, 8 ; I Pet.
ii, 9 ; II Pet. i, 3, 5]. One might perhaps say that
in the Pastoral Epistles the idea of truth was taken
from Hellenistic ethics and given a higher, Christian
meaning. Righteousness receives special attention in
the Pastorals because of their emphasis on the ethical
over against the gnostic. Ephesians has a liturgical
phrase (iv, 24) which describes the Christian as a new
man, " created in righteousness and holiness of truth "

(cf. Luke i, 75). The two clearest reminders of the Greek lists of virtues are at I Tim. vi, 11 and II Tim. ii, 22, where righteousness is one among other marks of Christian behaviour ; but the contents of these Christian lists differentiate them fundamentally from those of Philo, etc.

V. JUSTIFICATION

THE verb δικαιόω comes from the adjective δίκαιος, and means " to set right " or " make valid " (as ἀκυροῦν means " to cancel ", etc.).

(*a*) Pindar, in the famous fragment quoted by Plato (Gorg. 484*b*), says that convention, king of men and gods, pronounces right what otherwise would be called an act of violence.[1] Plato here sees natural right coming to its own ;[2] according to nature, might is right.[3] Philo often uses the word for the divine ordinance in the Law ; Josephus does so once (Ant. iv, 278) ; and the Passive Participles mean " prescribed " in Dion. Hal. Ant. Rom. X, i, 2 and Pap. Tebt. II, 444.

(*b*) From the legal sphere δικαιοῦν comes into general use to denote holding a thing to be right, reasonable, suitable. This is its commonest meaning, being found in Philo and Josephus as well as in classical authors. (For Paul's δικαιοῦν Josephus has ἀγαπῆσαι with the Genitive.[4]) Epictetus does not use the word at all.

(*c*) Applied to persons, δικαιοῦν is widely used for doing justice, and so comes to mean passing sentence (Thuc. III, 40), punishing (Herodot. I, 100),

---

[1] δικαιῶν τὸ βιαιότατον. U. von Wilamowitz, Platon II (1920), 93, 99, adopts the reading βιαιῶν τὸ δικαιότατον, " doing violence to what is most just ". Cf. J. Geffcken, Studien zu Plat. Gorg. in Herm. 65 (1930), 19. A. Busse, in Herm. 66 (1931), 126 ff., argues convincingly for the old reading. [2] Cf. Laws III, 690*c* ; IV, 715*a*.

[3] Cf. A. Busse, 127 f. [and R. W. Wenley, E.R.E. III, 242].

[4] Cf. Schlatter, Wie sprach Jos. von Gott ? (1910), 63.

executing (Jos. Ant. xvii, 206), defending (Polyb. III,
31). The last comes nearest to Paul's usage, but it is
only in LXX and N.T. that it means justifying a
person.

(d) The mystical use of the word in the Hermetic
tractate on Regeneration (Corp. Herm. xiii, 9)
claims special attention : χωρὶς γὰρ κρίσεως ἰδὲ πῶς
τὴν ἀδικίαν ἐξήλασεν. ἐδικαιώθημεν, ὦ τέκνον, ἀδικίας
ἀπούσης.[1] The formula means " we have become
sinless ", and may be intended to recall Christian
teaching. Righteousness is imparted to the initiate,
ἀδικία being banished by the annihilation of all evil
bodily desires (see p. 27). The absence of the idea
of judicial acquittal may be intended to counter the
Jewish-Christian view of justification. Perhaps it is
a presentation on the mystical plane of the Egyptian
idea of justification by means of the judgment of
the dead,[2] according to which the [heart of the]
dead man is weighed in the scales in the presence of
Osiris, and absolution depends on good works and
knowledge, faults being cleared away by magic.[3]

2. Δικαιόω IN THE SEPTUAGINT, ETC.

Δικαιοῦν in LXX, like its Hebrew equivalents
hiçdiq and çaddeq, is a forensic term, always favourable

[1] Reitzenstein, Poim, 343 ; Scott, I, 244. Cf. Reitzenstein,
Hell. Myst. 258 ff. ; C. F. G. Heinrici, Die Herm.-Myst. u. d.
N.T. (1918), 37. [But C. H. Dodd, The Bible and the Greeks,
1935, pp. 58 f., urges that the reference is to " an ethical
change ".]

[2] Reitzenstein, Hell. Myst. 258, also recalls the Persian
Judgment of the Dead, and the rather different Mandaic ideas.

[3] The Egyptian equivalent for " he is justified " is " his voice
is true ", this being decided by weighing the heart against a
feather, after forty-two questions have been answered, concerning behaviour during life. Cf. Erman-Grapow, Wörterb.
d. äg. Spr. (1926-31), II, 2 f., 22, 15 ; III, 324 ; J. H. Breasted,
Hist. Anc. Eg. (1908), 149.

in meaning (absolve, justify, vindicate). Its object is always personal. Sometimes it is more explicitly forensic than the Hebrew (e.g. Is. xlv, 25). The following uses should be noted.

Active. (*a*) For *hiçdiq* : acquit, pronounce righteous, secure justice—always for those who are righteous (I Kings viii, 32), never for the wicked (Exod. xxiii, 7).

(*b*) For *çaddeq* : show to be righteous (Jer. iii, 11).

(*c*) For *ribh* : get justice done for (Is. i, 17).

(*d*) Rarely for *zikkah* : cleanse (Ps. lxxiii, 13, LXX lxxii, 13). This word is very common in Rabbinic, meaning " pronounce righteous " : God does so on the Day of Atonement, making a man " a new creature " (Pesiqta Rabbati [9th cent.], 40, 169*a*) ; at death (Bab. Erub. 19*a*) ; or at the Last Judgment, on the ground of a preponderance of good works (see pp. 32 f., and cf. Midr. Ps. cxliii, 1, 266*b* ; Targ. Ps. li, 4, Heb. 6).[1] Justification is for the righteous, but evidently there is much uncertainty about it.[2]

(*e*) Rarely also for *shaphaṭ* : judge (I Sam. xii, 7, A ; B has δικάσω).

(*f*) Ps. Sol. never uses the word for justifying man, but only for recognising the justice, etc. of God (ii, 16, etc.). Cf. Luke vii, 29 (see p. 59). The same idea is often expressed in Rabbinic by *hiçdiq* or *çiddaq* (Bab. Ber. 19*a* ; Sifre Deut. 307 on xxxii, 4 ; Sifra Lev. on x, 3).

Passive. (*a*) To be shown to be righteous, to be justified—of God (Ps. li, 4 LXX l, 6 ; cf. Od. Sol. xxxi, 5—of the face of the Christ)[3] or of man (Ps. cxliii, LXX cxlii, 2). In the last example LXX is more

---

[1] Cf. Bill. III, 134 f. ; I, 640 f. ; Schlatter, Matt. 375.
[2] Cf. Bill. III, 134, 186 ff.   [3] [See D.A.C., II, 374*b*.]

sweeping than the Hebrew, and influences Paul in his doctrine of justification (Gal. ii, 16 ; Rom. iii, 20), though he always adds " by works of the Law ". In Ecclus. the Passive means " to be guiltless ", being in one place the equivalent of *niqqah* Niph. (xxxi, LXX xxxiv, 5). This usage is frequent in the Greek translations of Job other than LXX.[1]

(*b*) LXX changes Heb. Active into Passive in Job xxxiii, 32. [This might be on theological grounds, because God alone can justify.]

(*c*) The Perfect Passive means " to be righteous " (Gen. xxxviii, 26 ; Ps. xix, 9 LXX xviii, 10). Cf. Protevang. Jac. v, 1, where the Part. means " justified " after the offering of sacrifice.

(*d*) For *zakhah* : to be legally innocent (Mic. vi, 11).

(*e*) For *çdhq* Hithpa. : to justify oneself (Gen. xliv, 16 ; cf. Ecclus. vii, 5 and Luke xvi, 15—see p. 22).

3. Δικαιόω IN THE NEW TESTAMENT

Δικαιοῦν in the N.T. almost always implies the forensic metaphor, as it does in the LXX. It never has the ordinary Greek sense of holding right and reasonable.

(*a*) Δικαιωθήτω (Rev. xxii, 11) [2] means " practise righteousness ". This is exceptional. [Cf. Gen. xliv, 16.]

(*b*) The justification of God (Luke vii, 29), Wisdom

---

[1] At. Tob. vi, 12 f. Sin. the reference is to civil right.

[2] This is the reading of 38, 79, 2020, Vulg. Cl., Ep. Lugd. (Eus. Hist. Eccl. v, 1, 58), [accepted by Zahn, in Nestle's Einf., 264 f., and Bebb, Studia Biblica ii, 209 f., but] rejected by Nestle [and Moffatt ; Charles thinks the ver. an interpolation]; Cyprian, Test. III, 23, has *justiora faciat*.

(Matt. xi, 19 ; Luke vii, 35),[1] Christ (I Tim. iii, 16), means recognition of the divine justice.[2] (The last example says this took place in the sphere of the Spirit, i.e. his Messiahship was confirmed through the resurrection.) The juridical reference is more marked in Rom. iii, 4 (Ps. li, 4).

(*c*) The self-justification of the lawyer (Luke x, 29) is on a lower plane, though it still echoes the forensic. That of the Pharisees (Luke xvi, 15) comes nearer to the ordinary N.T. usage, suggesting, as it does, the usurping of the divine prerogative of judgment.

(*d*) Justification in the sense of being saved, with a definitely forensic reference, is found in the Synoptic Gospels, as well as in Paul. The publican (Luke xviii, 14) is judicially absolved on the spot,[3] the only difference from Paul being that there is no reference to the Cross.[4] Matt. xii, 37 speaks only of the Last Judgment (see p. 64).[5]

---

[1] P. de Lagarde, Agathangelos, A.G.G., 35 (1888), 128, suggested that the original Aramaic word, '*bdyh*' or '*bdy*', could be pointed so as to mean either " servants " or " works ". But Luke would hardly have used τέκνα for " servants ". If Schlatter, Matt. 374 f., were right in giving the verb its Hellenistic sense (condemn), we should have to regard this as pre-Lucan, since elsewhere in Luke the verb always has the positive meaning. The preposition ἀπό with " works " means " because of " ; with " children " it means " by " (for ὑπό, cf. Matt. xvi, 21 ; James i, 13) ; it is unnecessary to translate it " far from " (Dibelius, Joh. d. Täufer (1911), 19), or " in the presence of " (Wellhausen, Matt. (1904), 55, for Aram. *min qᵒdham*). The " works " denote not only the asceticism of the messengers, but the whole of their life.

[2] Cf. Bill. I, 604. See p. 58 for Ps. Sol. and Rabbinic. Euthymius ad loc. (M.P.G. cxxix, 357*c*) : δικαία καὶ ἀνέγκλητος ἐλογίσθη. Similarly, Jos. (Schlatter, Matt. 375 f.).

[3] Bill. II, 247 f.

[4] For the text, see Nestle. Παρ' ἐκεῖνον is exclusive and not comparative. Cf. II Esdr. xii, 7 : *prae multis*.

[5] Rabbinic par. in Schlatter, Matt. 412.

(e) Paul's doctrine of justification requires fuller treatment.

(i) The forensic idea is here clear and indisputable ; the opposite of δικαιοῦν is κατακρίνειν (Rom. viii, 34). What Paul has in mind is not the infusion of a moral quality, *justum efficere* in the sense of creating a life of righteousness, but the absolution and acquittal of the wicked, when he becomes a believer, on the ground of God's justifying action in the death and resurrection of Christ. This is certainly an act of mercy, not a judicial award according to works ; but it can still be called forensic, because on the Cross as ἱλαστήριον [Rom. iii, 25] all sin is finally judged in our representative.[1] Paul's originality lies in his use of δικαιοῦσθαι to denote that which God does as saviour now—leaving open the question of the relation of this to the Last Judgment, in which he still believes (see pp. 50 f.). The most thorough-going presentation of the matter is at Rom. iv, 5 ff., where Abraham is said to believe on " him that justifieth the ungodly " —in plain contradiction of the civil justice which justifies the righteous (cf. p. 58) ; the contrast is obviously intentional between an incomprehensible act of grace and conventional legality. Paul's "justification " is the effectual pronouncement of absolution now by the judge as saviour. It is neither absolutely objective in the Cross nor absolutely subjective in the experience of the believer ; its objectivity is relative—effectual in the Cross and realised in faith (see pp. 47-49). It is sometimes denied that the

[1] J. T. Beck, Rom. (1884), 217-223, limits the forensic references to the Last Judgment, as in O.T. and Rom. ii, 13, rejecting the judicial aspect of the Cross (222), where God is Father but not Judge. But this is contradicted by Paul's usage ; he loves to clothe God's act of forgiveness in forensic imagery. [On ἱλαστήριον see C. H. Dodd, Romans (1932), 54 f. and J.T.S. XXXII, 352-360.]

judicial act belongs to the present course of the religious life and can only mean the Last Judgment.
This would mean translating δικαιωθῆναι (Gal. ii,
16 f.) " become righteous in the sight of God " ;
justification would mean that the sinner receives from
God the status of a righteous man.[1] This is a legiti-
mate interpretation, but it should be added that the
new status is the result of a judicial pronouncement.

It may be admitted that the forensic reference is
not always made explicit by stressing the judicial act.
Thus οἵτινες ἐν νόμῳ δικαιοῦσθε (Gal. v, 4) means
simply " ye who fundamentally want to be righteous
through the Law ". But the whole argument is
haunted by the judicial idea, which again and again
receives impressive formulation : e.g. Gal. iii, 11 ; cf.
Rom. iii, 20 (from Ps. cxliii, LXX cxlii, 2). All
becomes obscure unless the main point is firmly held,
viz., that the forensic act is effectual in the act of
salvation, and is bound up with it. Only so can the
value of the new doctrine be seen, in comparison
with the Rabbinical view of justification, which
postpones the judicial act until the Last Judgment.
On the other hand, the forensic objectivity of the
saving act is endangered when supreme importance is
attached to the experience of the believer.

(ii) Paul's use of the verb δικαιοῦσθαι throws light
on the problem of experience, to which reference has
just been made. The present immediacy of justification is typically represented by a verbal " Present "
at Gal. iii, 8, 11, cf. ii, 16 and iii, 24 ; Rom. iii, 24,
26, 28, cf. Acts xiii, 39. " Past " forms are just as
important for our purpose (see p. 63, n. 3), because
they treat being justified as something which happens
at a given time, as an event. But to concentrate

---

[1] Zahn, Gal., 124 f. He agrees with Beck (see preceding note).

exclusively on the experiential aspect, in opposition
to the view that δικαιοῦσθαι means the act of universal
salvation perfected in the death of Christ,[1] is to
overlook the fact that this is the very event which
makes salvation continually present in actuality, and
thereby makes the personal attitude possible. The
latter is of course indispensable. Wherever justification is being discussed, faith must be included.[2]
It is impossible to separate justification once for all in
the Cross from personal justification in faith (see p. 48).
The locale of justification is the saving act (Rom. v, 9).
The historic Cross is the ground of salvation now.
" Being justified by faith " (Rom. v, 1) is the conse-
quence of " our justification " (iv, 25). What this
means cannot be truly or adequately stated in a formula
which is limited to the experiential aspect of the
matter ; the Cross and its work in the soul are too
closely bound up together ; it is impossible to con-
template the one without the other. The Past form
of the verb certainly expresses the completion of the
act of granting pardon.[3] But the addition of the
word " faith " (ἐκ πίστεως : Gal. iii, 8, 11, 24 ; Rom.
iii, 30 ; v, 1 ; or διὰ πίστεως : Gal. ii, 16) should
correct any tendency towards isolating the mere experience, since it necessarily implies a connexion with

[1] Zahn, Rom. 179 f., 209 n.17, 258.

[2] Gal. ii, 16 (twice) ; iii, 8, 11, 24 ; Rom. iii, 28, 30 ; iv, 5 ;
v, 1.

[3] See I Cor. vi, 11 ; Rom. iv, 2 ; v, 1, 9 ; Tit. iii, 7. The
genuine Paulinism of the last is questioned by Dibelius *ad loc.*,
but justification is associated with baptism here as at 1 Cor.
vi, 11 (see p. 47), and the connexion with inheritance and the
Spirit is thoroughly Pauline. Joh. Weiss's reference to Corp.
Herm. XIII, 9 (see p. 57) in explanation of I Cor. vi, 11 is
misleading, and is expressly disputed by Reitzenstein (Hell.
Myst. 259) ; he overlooks both Paul's dependence on the O.T.
and his view of the Christian's continual warfare with the flesh.
Cf. Gal. ii, 17 ; Phil. iii, 9.

the saving event. The tense of the verb in Rom.
viii, 30 does not mean that justification is past and
gone ; [1] the string of Aorists signifies that God's
eternal purpose has now been fulfilled. This leads to
the decisive point in connexion with the time-process :
the division between past and present is brought to
an end, so to speak, by the eternal quality of the
event which justifies and saves. That event remains
a continuing present.

(iii) The idea of justification according to works at
the Last Judgment finds expression at I Cor. iv, 4
(cf. Matt. xii, 37) : judicial approval and absolution
in the full sense can only be given when a man's
whole life is under review. That is evidently a different
use of the term from the one which we have been con-
sidering. It shows that Paul continued to associate
justification with the Last Judgment. The question
whether he expresses this idea elsewhere cannot be
settled by reference to cases in which he employs
Future forms of the verb δικαιόω. The example in
Gal. ii, 16 ; Rom. iii, 20 (see pp. 49-51) is not decisive, because the word occurs in a quotation (see
p. 62), but it may be presumed that Jews would take
it as pointing to the Last Judgment (see pp. 32 f.). The
context of Rom. ii, 13 shows that it cannot be regarded
as a complete statement of Christian belief, though
it maintains an abiding principle of divine judgment ;
it is one of a series of premises in an extended argument. The time-process is implied in Rom. iii, 30 ;
v, 19 ; viii, 33 ; the words are both logical [2] and
eschatological : the divine absolution of sins, made
effectual in the Cross and accepted by faith here
and now, is expected to reach its final consummation
in acquittal at the Last Judgment (see pp. 49-51).

---

[1] Zahn, Rom. 209 (" vergangener ").
[2] Lipsius, Zahn, Kühl, on Rom. v, 19.

Elsewhere Paul speaks of hope as the guarantee of present redemption (Rom. viii, 24).

(iv) The note of redemption is struck when the preposition ἀπό is used with the verb δικαιωθῆναι (cf. Ecclus. xxvi, 29 ; Test. Sim. vi, 1). This appears in the speech attributed to Paul in Acts xiii, where vv. 38 f. refer to forensic acquittal. (To say that the words imply the admission of a partial justification through the Law is an example of *Tendenz* criticism.[1]) What looks like an erratic boulder is found at Rom. vi, 7 : " He that hath died is justified from sin ". But this is a Rabbinical cliché, found, e.g., at Sifre Numb. 112 on xv, 31 (*kol hammethim bammithah mithkappᵉrim*) and implied in the doctrine of atonement through martyrdom.[2] Paul applies the saying to the Christian who has died with Christ, and is thus freed from his bondage to sin. The real point of his argument is conformity, through faith, with Christ's death, which holds the secret of justification. Comparison with the Rabbinic parallel is valuable as showing how Paul brought justification and atonement together ; it adds confirmation to the doctrine that justification rests on " propitiation " (ἱλαστήριον).[3]

[1] As in F. Overbeck, Kurze Erkl. der Ap. gesch. (1870), following Baur, and Preuschen, Ap. gesch. (1912). [" Critics advocate two interpretations : (i) the ὧν οὐκ ἠδυνήθητε, etc. means that by the Law of Moses acquittal of some things was possible, but not of others, and Paul was announcing this possible method of going beyond what the Law could do ; (ii) ὧν, etc., merely qualify πάντων, ' forgiveness for everything—which the Law never offered '. The former view is possible, but the latter seems more natural " (K. Lake and H. J. Cadbury, The Beginnings of Christianity, 1933, I, iv, 157).]

[2] First proved by K. G. Kuhn, Rom. vi, 7, Z.N.W., 30 (1931), 305 ff., to have been current in the first century A.D. See Horovitz (1917), 121, 13.

[3] It also makes it unnecessary to refer to the magical and mystical ideas of Corp. Herm. XIII, 9 (Reitzenstein, 259 f.). [For ἱλαστήριον see p. 61 n.]

(*f*) James uses the formula, "justified by works", three times [ii, 14 ff.], meaning justification here and now, and supports the doctrine with the examples of Abraham and Rahab. Paul denies this in the case of Abraham (Rom. iv, 2), but James is fighting against a form of orthodox monotheism that is ethically lifeless, and insists that faith without works cannot achieve justification (see p. 39). The problem of faith and works, and the terminology of the discussion, remind us of Paul, but there is no need to think that they come from him, or that this is a polemic against pseudo-paulinism or a misunderstanding of Paul. The similarity is due to the fact that both writers were familiar with the Rabbinical tradition. What is note-worthy is their agreement with the general view of the early Church that true faith is not an excuse for idleness, but a stimulus to work (see p. 40).

4. Δικαίωμα [1]

(*a*) Outside the New Testament this verbal noun, with the termination signifying result, has five meanings.

(i) Legal argument, plea, claim (Thuc. I, xli, 1 ; II Sam. xix, 28 LXX ; Jer. xi, 20 ; Jos. Ant. xix, 285 ; Jos. Ap. ii, 37 ; and often in Papyri).

(ii) Written evidence, deeds, minutes, etc., specially those in favour of the defence (Aristot., Fragm. p. 427

---

[1] See Cremer-Kögel ; Moulton-Milligan ; Zahn Rom., 278 f. ; Sickenberger Rom., 4th ed., 216 ; Rohr Heb., 4th ed., 40. Definitions : Aristot., Rhet. I, xiii, 1373*b*, 20 ff. ; Eth. Nic. V, x, 1135*a*, 9-14 ; Pseudo-Justin, Quaest. et Resp. ad Orth., III, ii, 138*c* (Otto) ; Origen Selecta in Ps. xviii (M.P.G. xii, 1244*c*).

Rose ; [1] Jos. Ant. xvii, 228 ; specially frequent in Papyri).[2]

(iii) Legal statute, ordinance, demand (often in LXX for *ḥoq*, *ḥuqqah*, Gen. xxvi, 5, etc. ; *mishpaṭ*, Exod. xxi, 1, etc. ; rarely for *miçwah*, Deut. xxx, 16 ; also in Philo, Josephus and Apostolic Fathers, the latter sometimes applying it to the Gospel, under the influence of the O.T. use of *çᵉdhaqah* (see p. 30)).

(iv) Judgment, sentence, condemnation (Plato Leg. IX, 864*e* ; I Kings iii, 28 ; viii, 45, 59 LXX). In Biblical usage it begins to mean a favourable verdict —like the verb.

(v) Right action, setting right, making good—the opposite of ἀδίκημα (Aristot. Rhet. I, iii, 1359*a*, 24 f. ; Eth. Nic. V, x, 1135 a 9-14 ; Theodoret on Ps. cxix (cxviii), 2 : νόμον καλεῖ . . . δικαιώματα, ὡς δικαιοῦν τὸν κατορθοῦντα δυνάμενον [3] ; Bar. ii, 29 : τὰ δικαιώματα τῶν πατέρων ἡμῶν).

(*b*) Three meanings of δικαίωμα are found in N.T.

(i) Most commonly it stands for "ordinance", illustrating the close adherence of N.T. to LXX, as in Luke i, 6 (see iii above). Paul, however, uses the word in the Singular, in a way which shows that he has gone deeper than LXX, and has the underlying principle in mind. Apart from Prov. viii, 20 and xix, 28 (25), LXX only means a particular ordinance by δικαίωμα, and usually has the Plural. Paul is concerned to show that the heathen also recognise a uniform moral order, according to which, by God's

---

[1] Cf. op. cit. 386 f. and ref. in Harpocration, Lexicon in Decem Oratores Atticos (Dindorf, 1853), s.v. δρυμός.

[2] Cf. A.P.F. VI, 1 (1913), 36 ; Moulton-Milligan and Preisigke s.v.—Dikaiomata, Auszüge aus alexandrin. Gesetzen u. Verordnungen, herausg. von der Graeca Halensis (1913), 26.

[3] Suidas, s.v., δικαιώματα.

decree, death is the penalty for perversion of worship
and social corruption (Rom. i, 32, where the word
may have the force of " condemnation "—see p. 67, iv).
There is a significant difference when the Plural
occurs at Rom. ii, 26. Then again, it is not accidental
that the Singular is found at Rom. viii, 4 [A.V.
righteousness ; R.V. ordinance ; R.V.m. require-
ment ; Tyndale, the rightewesnes requyred of the
law ; Moffatt misses the point with " requirements "],
where Paul is speaking of the fulfilment of the Law as
a whole by walking according to the Spirit. There is
no reference to the underlying principle at Heb.
ix, 1, 10, where the Plural has the same force as in
LXX.

(ii) Another meaning of δικαίωμα in the N.T. is
" righteous act ". In this sense it is attributed to
God (Rev. xv, 4, referring to his judgments, cf. Rom.
i, 32 and see iv and v above, p. 67) ; to the saints,
the members of the Church (Rev. xix, 8) ; and to
Christ. The last requires fuller discussion.

Whereas in Rom. v, 16 (see p. 70) it is contrasted
with κατάκριμα, condemnation, in ver. 18 its opposite is παράπτωμα, trespass (ruin as result), and this
is explained by the paraphrase in ver. 19, where the
contrast is between obedience and disobedience.
" One " in ver. 18 must be read as masculine, as it
is in the other ten cases of its occurrence in vv. 12-19,
referring to Adam and Christ respectively : " As one
man's trespass issued in doom for all, so one man's act
of redress issued in acquittal and life for all " [Moffatt].[1]
This harmonises with what Paul says elsewhere, viz.,
that the Christ, put under the Law (Gal. iv, 4), not
only knew no sin (II Cor. v, 21) in the sense of per-

---

[1] So e.g., Hofmann, Zahn, Lietzmann. It is taken as neuter
by Althaus, N.T. Deutsch [and by Sanday and Headlam].

sonal wrong-doing, but also, positively, was obedient
even unto death (Phil. ii, 8). All that is included in
the single formula which sums up the whole of his life
as δικαίωμα, perfect realisation of the righteous will of
God (cf. Matt. iii, 15 ; see p. 35).[1]

The other interpretation, which renders δικαίωμα
"pronouncement of justification",[2] though consistent with the rendering of the word in the rest of
this passage, breaks down on the fact that it presents
no true parallel to παράπτωμα, and this is absolutely
necessary. It also involves taking ἑνός as neuter
[agreeing with δικαιώματος], for the pronouncement
of justification is nowhere else by Paul ascribed to
Christ.[3] But the most serious difficulty lies in the
last three words of the verse : εἰς δικαίωσιν ζωῆς.
If δικαίωμα means the sentence of justification, we
are compelled to think that Paul here distinguishes
between the objective sentence and the individual
justification.[4] But there is no support for this in any
of the apostle's other utterances on the subject (see
pp. 47 and 62 ff.) ; God's justifying action (which on
this view would have to be the meaning of δικαίωμα in
ver. 18) is always represented as being actualised in the
faith of the believer.

[1] Cf. Zahn on Rom. v, 18. The parallels given above pre-
clude limitation to the Cross, though its centrality is thoroughly
Pauline ; cf. Phil. ii, 8, where, however, obedience is " even
unto ", not " only in " death.

[2] B. Weiss, Godet, Schlatter, Kühl, the last preferring " legal
arrangement " (Rechtsordnung)—but this is too formal.

[3] Consequently K. Barth suggests " the absolution made
known in the one ", but this is not a precise rendering.

[4] Godet and Lipsius (δικαίωσις, the actual pronouncement,
δικαίωμα, its content). But Rom. v, 16, the only place where
Paul unquestionably uses δικαίωμα for the pronouncement,
shows, by the contrast with κατάκριμα, that it is immediately
realised in the fullness of its working power.

(iii) The pronouncement of justification[1] is what δικαίωμα means in Rom. v, 16, where it is called a free gift and contrasted with condemnation. This is practically the same as δικαίωσις, the act of justification. A comparison of the use of the two words shows how easily the meaning fluctuates between punishment, claim, demand, ordinance, and when δικαίωμα means "righteous act" it includes elements of redress and reparation, which bring it very close to vindication (δικαίωσις ; see p. 71, ii). No doubt the exceptional use of δικαίωμα in Rom. v, 16 is partly to be explained on the ground of style, as being due to the presence in the same verse of 5 (6) other words ending in -μα.[2] Paul thus agrees here with the LXX usage (see p. 67, iv and cf. pp. 29 and 57).

The fact that δικαίωμα has so many different shades of meaning explains what is at first sight surprising—the use of the word in two senses in neighbouring verses (Rom. v, 16, 18) ; there is no reason to object to this, insisting on uniformity, since in each case the contrasted word makes the sense perfectly clear, and Paul elsewhere uses other connotations of this comprehensive term (Rom. i, 32 ; ii, 26 ; viii, 4).

5. Δικαίωσις

(a) General Greek literature employs this word to indicate five different aspects of putting into action that which is δίκαιον (right). It only occurs rarely, and is not found in Polybius, Philo,[3] Epictetus, or in any Papyrus or Inscription.

---

[1] Fritzsche, Meyer, Philippi, Godet, Barth, etc. Beck's "righteous standing" is impossible.

[2] Lietzmann, Rom. 60 ; Preuschen-Bauer, 308.

[3] The reading δικαίωσις for δεξίωσις (Deus. Imm. 79) makes no sense.

(i) The commonest meaning is condemnation, punishment (Thuc. VIII, lxvi, 2 ; [1] Jos. Ant. xviii, 14).

(ii) Judicial vindication and justification (Lysias ix, 8).[2] Paul uses the word in this sense. It also means self-vindication, justification of action taken in daily life (Plut., De Virt. Mor. 9 (II, 449b)).

(iii) Claim to real or apparent right (Thuc. I, cxli, 1).

(iv) Arbitrary decision (Thuc. III, lxxxii, 4). See p. 56 (b).

(v) Right (Plut., De Fort. 5 (ii, 99c) ; Lev. iv, 22 LXX for mishpaṭ).

Comparable expressions in Rabbinic are " pronouncement of judgment unto life " and " sentence of death " ('eyppophṣiṣ shel ḥayyim and 'eyppophṣiṣ shellahem lᵉmithah—Greek ἀπόφασις).[3] These are opposed to each other in Jer. Rosh Hash. 57a, 49.[4] Cf. bᵉshalom (in peace), ib. 59c, 51,[5] and bᵉdhimmuṣ (in acquittal [Latin dimissus]), Pesiqt. 155b,[6] both as the result of the divine judgment.

(b) Δικαίωσις is only found twice in N.T., Rom. iv, 25 ; v, 18, and means the act of justification through God's absolving judgment, which affects the whole of man's religious existence.

[1] Not equivalent to δικαιολογία, ἀπολογία (Cremer-Kögel, 332), but to κόλασις, as the scholiast has it (Hirzel, 138 ; cf. Liddell and Scott, s.v. ; Harpocration, s.v.).

[2] Harpocration, s.v.

[3] Cf. S. Krauss, Gr. u. lat. Lehnwörter in Talm. u. Midr. II (1899), 101 f. [4] Bill. III, 230 f. [5] Ib. 217 f.

[6] Ib. 218. [Cf. L. N. Dembitz, Acquittal in Talmudic Law, in J.E. : " Death-sentences were rare " ; Makkoth i, 10 : " A Sanhedrin that puts one man to death in a week of years is called bloody. Rabbi Eliezer ben Azariah says, Or one in even seventy years. Rabbi Tarfon and Rabbi Aqiba say, Had we been in the Sanhedrin none would ever have been put to death. Rabban Simeon ben Gamaliel says, They would even have multiplied the shedders of blood in Israel."]

Rom. iv, 25 says Christ " was delivered up for our trespasses, and was raised for our justification ", the preposition indicating cause in the first clause and purpose in the second. To take the second διά also as causal,[1] and translate, " because we have been justified ", leaves out of account the Abraham parallel, in which justification is the result of faith in God who quickeneth the dead [ver. 17]. It is rather that justification is brought about through the resurrection, which is so impressively connected with the faith of Abraham. It has been suggested [2] that the clause means that the resurrection is necessary for the real-isation of justification, since it first produces faith, which needs as its object more than one who has merely died. In reply to this it may be said that Paul does not construct his arguments in this fashion ; he prefers to say " much more " (Rom. v, 9) or " rather " (viii, 34). Christ's death and resurrection are inseparable in the N.T. ; the Crucified is what he is, only because he rose again ; and so Paul can say both that we are justified through his death, and that he was raised for our justification. Both the matter itself and the form in which it is stated are properly defined as synthetic parallelism.[3] One single idea is presented here in parallel expressions, while the reference to Abraham lays special emphasis on " was raised ".

Rom. v, 18 ends with the words, " to justification of life ", reiterating that God's pronouncement of justification is realised through the absolution of the believer. Justification and life are correlative, the former having perfect life as its content and making a present of it to the believer, so that it goes on working

---

[1] Lipsius, Rom., 2nd ed. (1892), 120.
[2] Zahn, Rom. 241 ; Kühl, Rom. 155 ff.
[3] J. Weiss, Beitr. zu paul. Rhet. (1897), 171.

in him eternally and is his final goal, just as condemnation is the end and outcome of transgression.
It is clear, from vv. 17 and 21, that " life " must be
understood eschatologically. But that it begins here
and now in him who is absolved, is proved, apart
from other arguments, by the use which Paul makes
of the term, " life ", in other places (Rom. vi, 4 ;
viii, 2, 6, 10). The phrase, " justification of life ",
therefore, like " be made righteous " in ver. 19,
confirms the observation that for Paul justification
looks forward to the perfecting through which alone
it receives its ideal (τέλος) and its final manifestation
(see pp. 49 ff. and 64).

6. Δικαιοκρισία only occurs once, in the eschatological setting of Rom. ii, 5. God's righteousness as
judge is contrasted with the moralising judgment of
those who condemn evil and yet do it themselves ;
" the judgment of God is according to truth " (ver. 2).
Cf. II Thess. i, 5, where the words " righteous " and
" judgment " are written separately, and the reference
is to the justice of the divine awards to persecutor and
persecuted respectively.

INDEX OF WORDS AND REFERENCES

(Scripture references are to the English Bible)